Animals' Rights

or

God's Rights

By

Coral Raven

Copyright © 2021 Coral Raven

ISBN: 9798723563766

A righteous man cares

for the needs

of his animals.

Proverbs 12

CONTENTS

Introduction

Appendix: Some Biblical Verses concerning Animal Sacrifice

References and Recommended Reading

Introduction

My main motive in writing this book comes out of a lifelong passion and love for animals. But it is also an expression of my grief and anguish concerning the killing of animals for any reason. I have, since a child, been disturbed at the thought of animals being slaughtered for meat. I just don't get how a farmer can keep animals, look after them and then let them go to a cruel death, for money. Neither do I understand how people consider it okay to kill an animal for food as long as the welfare of the animal leading up to slaughter is good. The killing itself is inhumane, whether behind closed doors in a slaughterhouse or out in the open in a bullring, it is morally wrong. It is abuse, exploitation, and unnecessary violence.

We draw an arbitrary line between species where we say dogs, cats and other pets should be cared for, but cows, pigs, chicken and fish have been defined as food animals, to be farmed for us to eat. We also rank them according to intelligence and make distinctions between which species is worthy of justice as opposed to others, according to how intelligent they are, their beauty or usefulness for making a profit. Animals do matter, they are not resources, property or commodities for us to use and abuse. Would God have given animals the ability to feel pain if he wanted us to eat them? They do have moral value, they are sentient beings just like us, they feel pain, they get scared, they smell death as they go into a slaughterhouse. Animal agriculture breeds animals into existence, they rape animals, they separate them from their families, and exploit them for their bones, their body, their flesh and their skin.

I will look at the environmental impact caused by factory farming and meat eating, despite concern for the environment not being my main interest, though I am glad that there is a recognition amongst environmental campaigners that meat eating is part of the problem. It is a catalyst in the stepping stones to a meat free society. Conservation is not my interest either. I have never been interested in conserving certain species or breeds of animals, not while we live in a world that is full of so much cruelty to animals. It is best that they are not born in the first place. Environmentalism and conservationism are not always compatible with a compassion and love for animals. It is human-centred.

I am not saying that we should not be concerned about the environment, I do believe there is a climate and environmental crisis which needs to be dealt with by governments and populations, particularly in industrial nations, such as the US, China, and Europe. Climate change can cause all sorts of worldwide problems, particularly in the poorest countries where it can cause migration because crops are not growing. Wealthy countries can adapt, but global displacement is at a high level currently. I would like to see the UK leading the way in making urgent changes in our lifestyles by each member of the public, with the Government introducing laws that enforce certain changes. We also need to build more renewable energy sources, such as wind farms; we are an island that could harness tidal and wind energy. We have the technology to use solar energy, wind energy, hydro energy and tidal energy.

My primary concern and reason for writing is to call us all to be compassionate towards God's creation, to partake in the divine nature of a God who extends His love to all creatures. If we wish to participate in the building of God's Kingdom, and carry out His will on earth as it is in Heaven, we need to ask ourselves is there killing going on in Heaven? I don't think so! We recite the words, "Thy Kingdom come, thy will be done, on earth as it is in heaven", so often as part of the Lord's Prayer, but do we really think about what we are saying?

Meat eating has become a conventional habit, tradition, and norm for centuries. The Bible has a part to play in this, in that so many passages talk about animals in the vein that it is perfectly acceptable to eat meat: animal sacrifices, talked a lot about in the Old Testament, are an example of this and many people see them as a justification to eat meat. So many scriptures that mention meat eating are often interpreted literally, whereas the actual meaning and purpose of the verse is metaphorical. In Romans 14:2 Paul wrote that those who eat only vegetables are weak. I am not so sure that this passage is about meat eating at all. It is about Christian maturity and our levels of faith. Some of us have stronger faith than others. My understanding of Romans 14 is that it is about walking in love and not judging one another. Are we really weak if we eat vegetables? Weak in what way, physically, spiritually? Hardly! Is it about what we feed off spiritually, meat being a metaphor for substance and the deeper things of God? Verse 17 clarifies, 'For the Kingdom of God is not a matter of eating and drinking, but of righteousness, peace and joy in the Holy Spirit'.

If you, the reader, disagree with me about Paul's opinions on this issue, and would prefer to think that Paul was actually talking about meat eating and vegetarians, I would ask you to consider whether Paul was a bit dismissive and shallow in his thoughts on this subject. Why doesn't he mention the welfare of animals, why doesn't he discuss in depth the rights and wrongs of killing an animal to eat as meat. He obviously had come across vegetarians and perhaps wondered why they choose not to eat meat. Perhaps they were even his 'thorn in the flesh'. I don't think Paul would have been a vegetarian. Writing to the Christians in Corinth, he told them, "Eat anything sold in the meat market". (1 Corinthians 10:25), though I think he

3

is referring here to the dietary laws against eating certain flesh foods, which were a subject of controversy in those times. James, the brother of Jesus was vegetarian and Paul must have come across the Essenes in his social and perhaps church circles. Vegans and vegetarians have always been a source of annoyance and they certainly are today, in fact in these current times more than ever, with organisations such as Extinction Rebellion, and other uprisings making their voices heard in a powerful way, with a determination that isn't going to go away.

Another favourite passage is Peter's vision in Acts 10 where he sees a sheet bound at four corners being let down from heaven, containing all kinds of animals. He heard a voice from Heaven saying kill and eat. But Peter refused saying he had never eaten anything common or unclean. The voice replied, 'What God has cleansed you must not call common.' Many readers of this scripture simplistically assume and interpret it literally to mean that God is telling Peter it is okay to eat what the Jews would regard as unclean meat.

There is far more substance and meaning going on in this story. The important point of the story is that Jews did not enter the home of a gentile, they were considered unclean. Peter was a Jewish Christian. Cornelius was a Gentile, and a godly man with a good reputation among the Jews. Later Peter meets Cornelius. God used the Jewish dietary laws to speak to Peter through this vision. Perhaps Peter's prejudice against what he saw as unclean, the gentiles, was an issue that God needed to deal with. God softened Peter's heart and lead him to Cornelius's house where there was a congregation of gentiles and Peter preached the gospel to them. While he did so the Holy Spirit fell on the gentiles, and they were baptized. This is the true meaning of Peter's vision. It was a vision from God to break through Peter's fears and prejudices to enable him to preach the gospel to the gentiles and to see them as equal. He says to Cornelius, "Stand up; I myself am also a man". (Acts 10:26)

Whatever your views may be regarding whether we should eat meat or not, some believe we have moved into a new age, and that it is the last age, where meat eating will be challenged and there will be no let up until it is abolished. Research is being done into producing good quality alternative foods, companies are already producing good meat free burgers which are as good, if not better, than a beef burger. One company is even attempting to produce meat from the cell of an animal, which will involve no killing of flesh at all. The quality of vegan and vegetarian foods in the supermarkets are improving, I have noticed the quality of the alternative plant-based milks are creamier with a higher quantity of nut or seed in the ingredients than there was previously. There is a lot of competition and increasingly new brands are appearing on our supermarket shelves offering a better quality of milk substitutes and vegan and vegetarian foods.

We are moving into a new age, from the church age to the Kingdom age, and I believe we have been in transition over the past ten years or so, and we have actually stepped into the next age in this decade of twenty-twenty. There are ages talked about in the biblical story of salvation. An excellent book has been written by Christopher Paul Carter entitled *Cosmic Shift,* who talks about the different ages, and he says that we are currently moving into the age of Aquarius, which is a new season of faith. I realise that the Age of Aquarius has been a 'New Age' concept for some time, there was even a song written about the age of Aquarius. The New-Agers were on to something and many Christians are waking up to the fact that the enemy has taken a truth and made it his own, Satan can only copy, he cannot create. Chris Carter states on the cover of his book, "I believe this next age can't possibly be grasped without understanding God's history with man and the story of

5

redemption. Conversely, the story of our redemption from sin and the fall can't be completely understood without a concept of how the ages change and the promise of a soon coming new age." He believes that all of humanity is passing through a grand cosmic gate, on its way to a new season of faith and a new season of light.

I believe that the end of meat eating will happen when this next age, or last age, is completely ushered in. We are, at the moment, in transition from the age of Pisces, the age of traditional church, church as we know it will be no more either. We will do things differently, there is a movement of Christian Mystics and Seers, who are already in the forefront and have embraced this next age, many of them had become bored with church as we have known it, and were seeking more, and yearning to know God, not just in knowledge and theology, but experiencing Him and His presence in their lives. There has been compromise and passivity in the church in the past, though there is a radical shift happening. Mystics are seeking to know God, to encounter Him in their daily lives, seeking intimacy with Him in relationship, they are seeing miracles happen, seeing in the spirit, going into Heaven by faith or the imagination, and some are experiencing getting caught up in the spirit into heavenly places.

The word 'mystic' sets off alarm bells for many old school Christians. However, the Bible talks about seeking the mystery of God, for example, Paul writing to the Colossians, expresses his desire to encourage and unite them in love, 'so that they may have the full riches of complete understanding, in order that they may know the mystery of God, namely, Christ, in whom are hidden all the treasures of wisdom and knowledge'. The church is moving from the prophetic to the mystic age. A mystic is someone seeking mystic union with the Godhead, by entering the torn veil, and seeking revelation of divine mysteries in heavenly places. The Book of Revelation

6

exhorts us to, 'come up here', and in Ephesians 2 tells us we are seated with Christ in the heavenly realms, in order that in the coming ages he might show the incomparable riches of his grace'. Mystics desire to live on earth now as it is in Heaven and to interact with Heaven.

These are exciting times in which we are living! I do hope this book will help those who are considering adopting a compassionate, plant-based diet, and that it may answer some questions you may have.

The question is not,
Can they reason?
Nor can they talk?
But can they suffer?
Why should the law refuse
protection to any sensitive being?

Jeremy Bentham (1789)

One

The Status of Animals

Do animals have rights, does man have rights? If we didn't have rights, there would be no justice system whose job it is to ensure that we have freedom and liberty without infringing the liberty of any other human being.

But what about animals, and what does God think about animals, fish, birds of the air and all the living creatures which He created. There are numerous expressions of God's love for His creation including animals throughout the scripture. Psalm 104 celebrates and gives thanks to the Lord for supplying all the needs of His creation, they look to Him to give them their food at the proper time and He satisfies them with good things. He enjoys animals just as we do. God has created such awesome wonder in the design of animals. He is the great creator! My vision of Heaven is of a place teeming with animals, all manner of fantastical creatures, I think we will be surprised. The four faces of God described in Ezekiel and Revelation around the Throne in Heaven are described as four living creatures covered with eyes, in front and behind. The first living creature is like a lion the second like an ox, the third had a face like a man, and the fourth was like a flying eagle.

In Matthew 10:29-31 when Jesus teaches on the fear and reverence of the Lord, he reassures us that we are loved, that we are of more value than the sparrows, He values them too. Animals praise God and bring glory to Him, in Psalm 148 we see all of creation praising the Lord. Psalm 150 exhorts us to 'Let everything that has breath praise the Lord'.

Animals have the capacity to enjoy life. Psalm 104 is a wonderful expression and picture of creation and God's provision for it, of how everything in and of the earth works together. In Job 39:13 God describes the ostrich flapping its wings joyously, and in Job 40:20 the beasts of the field are playing in their surroundings. He even created the Leviathan to play in the sea (v.26). We have all seen animals playing, and it is a joy to watch them. Just as we are here for God's pleasure and will (Ephesians 1:5), so are the animals. They are also an expression of His glory just as we are.

You may ask, but do they have a soul, as we do. Ecclesiastes asks the same question and concludes that we all have the same breath and that man has no advantage over the animal, though he doesn't know the destiny of their spirit. Concerning the question of whether animals have souls and spirits, being brought up in a Christian household, I had always been dogmatically told that they do not, and so accepted this belief as absolute truth. But I have wondered more recently, why on earth God would create all the wonderful and varied creatures that we enjoy around us. It seems arrogant and anthropocentric for Christians to claim that only humans have souls.

Do animals have feelings? In the same way that humans show emotions in their eyes, whether happiness or sadness, I often see sadness in a person's eyes resulting from sadness and grief that has happened to them in the past. I see the same in the eyes of animals. I see expressions in the eyes of dogs, one can see what type of life they have had, and what type of homelife they may have now. For example, when I am out walking, or out shopping in the streets of Chichester, where there are plenty of dogs with their owners, I have seen in the eyes of some of them, such emotions as contentment, fear, happiness, excitement, sadness, and unhappiness. I think we have known for a long time that animals feel emotions just like we do. Why do we need the evidence and word of proof from scientists to back up every theory that we instinctively already know to be true, and has actually been proven by the experiences of animal behaviourists and the experiences of anyone who observes and lives with a pet? There are many stories of the loyalty of dogs to their owners even in death. There seems to be a reluctance amongst scientists to admit that animals have emotions, though they are gradually beginning to accept that humans are not the only species with the capacity to feel emotions. In an article written in the Daily Mail, dated 2 January 2020, entitled, 'Who says animals don't have feelings', the author Frans de Waal, states that, 'The possibility that animals experience emotions like humans do makes hard-nosed scientists feel queasy'. He goes on to say, 'But of course it has long suited us to assume that animals are dumb automatons devoid of feelings and awareness, as science has done for a long time. That they are not, presents us with a serious moral dilemma, and in this era of factory farming, animal sentience is, you might say, the elephant in the room'.

I think the reluctance by scientists, who tend to act as our moral map in society, to speak out and declare that animals do feel pain, they do suffer, they do feel emotions, including happiness, is of huge significance. It they were to do so, the implications would be profound, it would become harder to subject animals to factory farming which would not be conducive to their happiness and wellbeing. It would have huge implications for meat-eaters, many of whom may be scientists. Denying that animals feel allows us to do whatever we want to them. Charles Darwin said, "Animals, whom we have made our slaves, we do not like to consider our equal".

People have their own opinions, but I believe that we will see animals in Heaven. Many people have seen creatures in Heaven. I also believe there are all sorts of weird and wonderful creatures in Heaven. I have seen tropical birds and monkeys in vivid greenery. I have also been taken up in the spirit in my sleep and saw a white horse. This may seem ridiculous to those readers who, firstly, view the subject of animals in the way that I discuss in this book from a contrary standpoint. Secondly, there will be those who are outraged at the idea of going into heaven now or having any kind of supernatural experiences. We are seated in the Heavenly realms in Christ Jesus (Ephesians 2:6) and we can go there at any time by faith or in the spirit. I do know people who regularly step into the realms of heaven in their everyday life, they step in and out of the different dimensions, just as Enoch did. Enoch walked with God daily, he experienced heaven and the glory of God in his life. There are many books written which relate the experiences of those who see open visions, get taken off in the spirit, and spend time with God in heavenly places, and know His presence in their lives.

I am writing with the firm belief that animals are sentient beings. It is clear to me that animals do feel pain and I do not feel that I need to convince the reader of this fact, particularly those who own pets. A dog, for instance, will yelp when in distress or feeling pain. We know that animals have a nervous system and that they react to pain just as we do.

The philosopher Jeremy Bentham asked: 'The question is not, can they reason? Nor can they talk? But can they suffer?" The subject of pain and suffering is a very important aspect when considering the status of animals. The capacity for suffering, as well as pleasure, is, 'the vital characteristic that entitles a being to equal consideration', according to Peter Singer in Practical Ethics. Animals are worthy of concern in their own right. Proverbs 12 declares, 'A righteous man cares for the needs of his animals'.

Compassion for animals has, throughout the centuries of time, been expressed by thinkers, by saints, writers and philosophers. Some were concerned about the welfare of animals and were against humans being cruel towards them and saw it as morally wrong, for example, John Locke (1632-1704), and Thomas Aquinas (1225-1274). But their concern was human centred because they believed that cruelty to animals desensitized their humanity. The German philosopher, Immanuel Kant argued in 1785 that, 'cruelty to animals is contrary to man's duty to himself, because it deadens in him the feeling of sympathy for their sufferings, and thus a natural tendency that is very useful to morality in relation to other human beings is weakened'. Contrary to these opinions, Jean-Jacques Rousseau acknowledges that the sentience of animals entitles them to not being ill-treated. Jeremy Bentham, an English philosopher (1748-1832) argued that it was the ability to suffer that gives the right to equal consideration.

The Reverend Professor Andrew Linzey, in his excellent book, *Why Animal Suffering Matters*, goes to great lengths to argue that animal suffering does matter. He maintains that special consideration and a special moral status should be accorded to animals and children. A change in people's perception of animals has to change from the conditioning of our thinking for centuries into seeing animals as something to eat, as commodities, resources, mere objects for us to use and abuse. I do believe it is happening, particularly among the younger generations, who are horrified like I was as a young child, that animals are killed to be eaten. Animals do have an intrinsic value, they matter and their suffering is important, people are beginning to actually see animals, they are waking up to the fact that they have value, rather than taking them for granted as being lower than us, to appreciate them as living being. There is a passive silence, a burying of the head in the sand, an acceptance of the status quo because it is easier, it is too difficult for some people to face the morality of causing animal suffering. For some, the status quo serves their interests because there is money and profit involved and they would have to make a radical change to their lifestyle and so resignation to the current situation is their choice. I would agree with Andrew Linzey, that animal abuse has been made socially acceptable and institutionalised, and this is what makes change so difficult. Noam Chomsky in his book *Media Control*, called it, 'controlling thought and manufacturing consent'. We all have been influenced by parental guidance, schooling, place of work, media, conventional ways of living and moral standards, and unless we are faced with the question of challenging traditions, we may continue to conveniently be ostrich-like in our avoidance of thinking about the issue of animal cruelty. We have become dulled in our thinking, we are influenced by the status quo of everything that goes on around us, we have become unconscious and generally live much of our lives drifting along in automatic, without questioning anything.

Another problem is that most of the cruelty that goes on is behind closed doors and, unless highlighted by the media, or animal welfare charities, we do not see beyond the sanitised packaging of our meat in the supermarket for instance. We do not see the animal being slaughtered, we imagine it to be humane, because that is what we are told and conditioned to think, but no form of killing by its very nature can be humane. We are not told about the inevitable abuse that happens in the slaughterhouses either, the kicking and loss of patience by the slaughter-men. For me, I cannot imagine anyone wanting to work in such a place, it is bound to brutalise that person, it is unnatural, it is after all killing a living being, and is going to make it easier for that person to kill a human being if they were so inclined. Some animal abuse, of course, may be a result of the actions of people who have a cruel tendency, and that will usually also manifest towards humans, and particularly towards children. I do believe there is a link between animal abuse and human violence.

In Genesis 1:26 God said:

Let us make man in our image, in our likeness and let them rule over the fish of the sea and the birds of the air, over the cattle, over all the earth, and over all the creatures that move along the ground.

This is certainly no licence to abuse God's creatures nor to use them as mere commodities, they are sentient beings. This should be understood as unselfish guardianship with love and compassion, not selfish power. Humans are to be as loving toward all of creation as God was in creating it. Those who respect the rights or welfare of animals are embarked on a journey back to Eden, a journey back to a proper love for God's creation. I cannot accept that God created animals merely for human use and consumption, that would be entirely out of character for a loving, compassionate and just God.

Animals have attributes that contribute and add richness to our lives. Anyone who owns a dog will notice their unique qualities and characteristics if they are paying attention. They have character and such values as love, goodness, enthusiasm, curiosity, dignity, happiness and fun. I believe we can communicate with the non-human species, that there is a universal language, that we can have kinship with all life. I know from having a dog myself that it could read my thinking, sense how I felt, and sense and no doubt see invisible things.

J Allen Boone has written a delightful book entitled Kinship with All Life. He conveys his real-life experiences with animals, one being a dog called Strongheart who he looked after for long periods while its owner was away on business, and his attempts to see and know him as he really was. He concludes, 'with the dog's guiding help, and with him as the focal point for the experience, I was receiving priceless primary lessons in the cosmic art of seeing things as they really are – through the mists and barriers that seem to separate all of us from one another'.

15

I think it is commonly accepted now that we can communicate with nature, and no I do not have an overactive imagination, nor am I crazy! Prince Charles admitted that he talks to his plants, and that was decades ago. There are energies and frequencies in nature and all around us within God's creation, within ourselves, animals, birds of the air and fish and all living things. Creation has sounds and is alive, if only we would take the time to listen. It is us humans that place limitations on animals just as we do children. We block the imagination of children by telling them it has no worth and is only airy-fairy imaginings. All life is able to speak with all life, whenever minds and hearts are properly attuned.

I want to establish at the beginning of this book that animals are not inferior, that they are intelligent and fellow beings and we can learn so much from them; God values them, he created them and he holds their breath, as he holds ours. Job recommended that we:

Ask the animals, and they will teach you, or the birds of the air, and they will tell you; or speak to the earth, and it will teach you, or let the fish of the sea inform you.

(Job 12:7)

I want to move away from the media's distorted portrayal, the manipulating propaganda that shapes our thoughts. Whenever a documentary is shown on the television regarding, for example, factory farming, the ethical or moral aspect of whether we should or shouldn't be eating meat is never tackled, it always comes from an environmental or commercial point of view, or how many jobs it can provide. Any discussion on fox hunting usually focusses on foxes being controlled because they are vermin, and again how many jobs would be lost if it was banned. It is all about utilitarianism, what is the usefulness and how does it benefit us, but where does morality or ethics come into the argument? Media discussions and documentaries on any topic are usually full of sound bites.

16

So, do animals have the same rights as humans? Human rights are defined and protected by law. They are based on values like dignity, fairness, respect and independence. I do believe they should have the same rights as humans, that is to be treated with equal consideration of interests. I have established that animals are sentient beings, are self-conscious and have the capacity for suffering as we do. All creatures are valued by God and His rights in creation are for us to recognise the duty we have to also value animals, to love them as God does. In Psalm 50, the Mighty One, God, the Lord declares:

I have no need of a bull from your stall or of goats from your pens, for every animal of the forest is mine, and the cattle on a thousand hills, I know every bird in the mountains, and the creatures of the field are mine.

Sacrifices and offerings,
Burnt offerings and sin offerings
You did not desire,
Nor were you pleased with them.
Hebrews 10:5

Two

I Desire Mercy, Not Sacrifice

Jesus stresses these words in various scriptures, that He desires mercy and not sacrifice, for example in Matthew 9:13, Matthews 12:7, Hosea 6:6. One of the most common questions often put to me regarding meat eating is concerning the Old Testament sacrifices. The thought held by many is that if God commanded sacrifices for the atonement of sins, then it must be okay to slaughter animals for food now. It is usually said in the tone that if God allowed sacrifices, even commanded them, He must allow meat eating. The assumption here is that God commanded and instituted the practice of the Levitical sacrifice.

It is clear throughout the scriptures, in so many verses, that God did not delight in the animal sacrifices practiced by His people. He hated it, he called it an abomination. Leviticus 1:2 says, 'When any one of you brings an offering.... '. The use of the word 'when' at the beginning of the sentence suggests it is a voluntary practice rather than an actual commandment. Jeremiah 6:20 states, 'Your burnt offerings are not acceptable, nor your sacrifices sweet to me.' Hosea 6:6, 'For I desire mercy, not sacrifice'. You may ask why does scripture say that God was pleased by the sweet-smelling aroma. Actually, this is not what verses such as Leviticus 1:9, Leviticus 2:2, and Leviticus 23:18 say. These and other verses talk of 'an offering made by fire for a sweet aroma to the Lord'. It doesn't say that the Lord says the aroma is sweet to Him, it is the person offering the sacrifice who considers it to be a sweet aroma!

19

Some sources say that the sacrificial system originated from pagan practices, and that it was never commanded by God. Even if you abide by the traditional religious belief that it was a commandment by God, that does not make it right to slaughter animals for meat now. I don't see a connection myself when there is so much written evidence in the scriptures and in ancient scripts stating that God detested the practice of sacrifice whether animal or human. One of the ten commandments, 'do not kill', surely includes animals.

Jeremiah 19: 3-5 depicts God's chosen people sacrificing their sons to the gods of Baal. He says, "I did not command or speak, nor did it come into my mind." God is speaking to rebellious people who are disobeying God. Circumcision was commanded in the Bible, or at least our translations of it, say so. It doesn't mean it is good or required right now in the time we live. I would even question whether God really did command such a barbaric practice. It is certainly no longer necessary, if it ever was, because we are under a new covenant. Hebrews 9:9 talks about the first tabernacle and how, 'the gifts and sacrifices being offered were not able to clear the conscience of the worshipper'. So why would God command animal sacrifices if they were of no avail and pointless? Nobody could sacrifice enough to satisfy the priests. All of their sacrifices did not bring the Utopia they desired. No, it bought nothing but destruction, suffering and genocide. The Hebrew people were betrayed by their own priests. Hebrews 10:4 says:

It is impossible for the blood of bulls and goats to take away sin, sacrifice and offering you did not desire, but a body you prepared for me; with burnt offerings and sin offerings you were not pleased. Then I said, 'Here I am – it is written about me in the scroll – I have come to do your will, O god'.

First, he said, "Sacrifices and offerings, burnt offerings and sin offerings you did not desire, nor were you pleased with them" (although the law required them to be made). Then he said, "Here I am, I have come to do your will.

God never desired animal sacrifice, and Jesus came and abolished them all. Was it His original intention? I don't think so, certainly not before sin and death came into the world through Adam's sin.

I list below some further scriptures which stress this point: Psalm 40:6, 'Sacrifice and offering you did not desire; my ears you have opened. Burnt offerings and sin offerings You did not require'. Psalm 51:16, 'You do not delight in sacrifice, or I would bring it, you do not take pleasure in burnt-offerings. These, O God, you will not despise'. The sacrifices of God are a broken spirit, a broken and contrite heart, but those who were performing animal sacrifices were wicked and sinful, and they failed to repent of their sins, and so their sacrifices were futile. Isaiah 1:11-13:

The multitude of sacrifices – what are they to me?" says the Lord. "I have more than enough of burnt offerings, of rams and the fat of fattened animals; I have no pleasure in the blood of bulls and lambs and goats. When you come to appear before me, who has asked this of you, this tramping of my courts? Stop bringing meaningless offerings! Your incense is detestable to me.

Isaiah 66:3 says:

He who kills a bull is as if he slay a man; He who sacrifices a lamb, as if he breaks a dog's neck; He who offers a grain offering, as if he offers swine's blood; He who burns incense, as if he blesses an idol.

Several prophets objected to sacrifice, emphasizing that God prefers righteousness. Jeremiah says in chapter 6:20, this is what the Lord says, "Your burnt offerings are not acceptable, your sacrifices do not please me". In chapter 7:21, the Lord gave another message to Jeremiah to give to the people at the entrance to the Lord's Temple, and clearly the Lord is angry with the people of Israel:

Add your burnt offerings to your sacrifices and eat meat. For I did not speak to your fathers, or command them in the day that I brought them out of the land of Egypt, concerning burnt offerings or sacrifices. But this is what I commanded them, saying, Obey My voice, and I will be your God, and you shall be My people. And walk in all the ways that I have commanded you, that it may be well with you. (NKJ version).

This is said in anger, in the same tone that he told Moses to tell the people of Israel to consecrate themselves in preparation for the next day when they would be allowed to eat meat. They had been complaining about the manna that the Lord had provided and kept calling out for meat. The Lord heard their wailing and complaints, and told Moses to tell them that He would give them meat, not just for one day, or two days, five, ten or twenty days, but for a whole month, until it came out of their nostrils and they loathe it. We see also in the New Testament a scene where Jesus shows his anger, in Matthew 21, Mark 11 and Luke 19 where Jesus entered the temple area and drove out all who were buying and selling there. He overturned the tables of the money changers and the benches of those selling doves.

The Church Father Epiphanius, writing in the 4th Century, makes a distinction between two main groups within the Essenes, the Ossaeans and the Nasaraeans. I am particularly interested in what he says about the Nasaraeans, because Jesus had lived in Nazareth. Matthew 2:23 reminds us of the fulfilment of the prophets, that, "He will be called a Nazarene". They were Jews by nationality who acknowledged Moses and believed that he had received laws, though not the laws they knew. They were Jews who kept Jewish observances, but they would not offer sacrifice or eat meat. They considered it unlawful to

22

eat meat or make sacrifices with it. They claim that none of those customs were instituted by the fathers.

In the Gospel of the Ebionites, Jesus rejects the Passover meat and attacks animal sacrifices saying, "I have come to destroy the sacrifices". (Ephinanius, Panarion 30.16.4 in The Homilies written by Clement). The Gospel of the Ebionites can be dated between the middle and end of the second century. There are eight fragmentary passages contained in Epiphanius' Panarion. The following is an extract where Kefa states in the Homilies of Clement (Chap. Xly):

But that He is not pleased with sacrifices, is shown by this: those who lusted after flesh were slain as soon as they tasted it, and were consigned to a tomb, so that it was called the grave of lusts. He then who at the first was displeased with the slaughtering of animals, not wishing them to be slain, did not ordain sacrifices as desiring them; nor from the beginning did He require them. For neither are sacrifices accomplished without the slaughter of animals, nor can the first-fruits be presented.

Egypt had a sacrificial system. Some scholars believe that the sacrificial system, found in the Pentateuch, was absorbed from the Canaanites, that it was developed under their influence. In 2 Kings 16, King Ahaz, who did not do right in the eyes of God, even sacrificed his own son following the detestable ways of the nations the Lord had driven out. In verse 10, King Ahaz went to Damascus to meet Tiglath-Pileser, king of Assyria. There he saw an altar, and he admired the design and so he sent to Uriah the Priest a sketch of the altar, with detailed plans for its construction. Uriah the Priest then built an altar in accordance with the design that King Ahaz had sent from Damascus. When King Ahaz saw the altar, he made offerings on it, burnt offerings and grain offering. So, the priests were allowing the kings to bring in these pagan practices.

Jeremiah speaks a lot against the sacrifices and the shedding of innocent blood both human and animal in the temple. Lamentations 4 talks about the iniquities of the priests who shed the blood of innocents, both human and animal. He reports that they are so defiled with blood that no one dares to touch their garments. Kefa claimed that some of the Torah, which was written by the priests, was corrupted. There is much controversy over the authorship of the Torah, some scholars think it was written by multiple authors at various times, written over centuries and that there are different document sources: J the Jahwist source, E the Elohist source, P the priestly source. Some argue that it consists of short independent narratives brought together in two editorial phases, the first Deuteronomic, the second Priestly. Others argue that the Torah was derived from a series of additions to an existing corpus of work. Most scholars agree that some form of priestly work existed and that the Torah consists of a fusion of sources over centuries by many authors. I am not going to argue a case because I don't know and suspect no one knows the truth concerning the authorship. Also new theories are always emerging. There are plenty of references for these documentary hypothesis and theories to be found on line.

When I study the Book of Leviticus, with its gory and bloody detail, about the bloodletting rituals, the sacrificial rites and dare I say superstitions, I struggle to believe that they are God ordained. They sound more like primitive pagan practices from distant primal ages. Even today a peculiar custom has developed around Yom Kippur which involves swinging a chicken over your head three times to absolve yourself of sin. What an absurd practice!

I am aware that the Lord instructed Moses and Aaron concerning the Passover, in Exodus 12, to tell the whole community of Israel that on the tenth day of the first month of their year, they must take a lamb for his family, a lamb without defect, and to put the blood on the sides and tops of the doorframes of the houses so that the Lord would pass over them and no destructive plague would touch them. This, of course, is figurative of the future coming of the lamb of God without blemish, who would be the great sacrifice bringing about salvation for mankind.

There are many events and practices in the Old Testament that are difficult for us to understand or accept such as animal sacrifice, circumcision, and the mass killings and wiping out of entire nations, things that are abhorrent and morally reprehensible to us now, all seemingly on God's instructions. Also, God may have tolerated certain practices, but would not have endorsed them. Paul, in Romans 11:33, acknowledges that God's judgements are unsearchable. God is a righteous God, and His wrath against sin must find an expression in judgment. Once we realise this, we can then appreciate God's amazing love displayed in the cross of Christ. Romans 5:8, God demonstrates His own love for us in this: While we were still sinners, Christ died for us. Also, we can begin to see why His death was necessary to demonstrate God's justice and avert God's wrath from us. Christ Jesus, the Lamb of God became the sacrifice of atonement once and for all which brought an end to animal sacrifice. So why do we persist in sacrificing animals by killing them for food?

We are meant to present ourselves as a living sacrifice unto Him, to put our faith and trust in the Lord that He has a good plan for our lives and will restore us to be the person He created us to be.

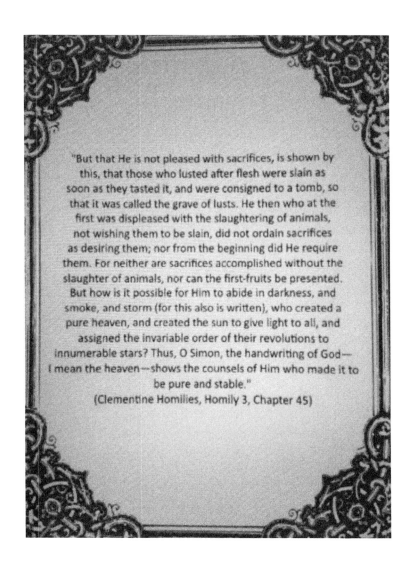

"But that He is not pleased with sacrifices, is shown by this, that those who lusted after flesh were slain as soon as they tasted it, and were consigned to a tomb, so that it was called the grave of lusts. He then who at the first was displeased with the slaughtering of animals, not wishing them to be slain, did not ordain sacrifices as desiring them; nor from the beginning did He require them. For neither are sacrifices accomplished without the slaughter of animals, nor can the first-fruits be presented. But how is it possible for Him to abide in darkness, and smoke, and storm (for this also is written), who created a pure heaven, and created the sun to give light to all, and assigned the invariable order of their revolutions to innumerable stars? Thus, O Simon, the handwriting of God—I mean the heaven—shows the counsels of Him who made it to be pure and stable."
(Clementine Homilies, Homily 3, Chapter 45)

How many are your works?
O Lord!
In wisdom you made them all;
The earth is full of your creatures.
Psalm 104

Three

Was Jesus Vegetarian?

James, the brother of Jesus, was a strict vegetarian. He was raised as a vegetarian (Eusebius, Ecclesiastical History 2.23.5-6). Why would Jesus' family raise James as a vegetarian, but not Jesus? The text of this ancient document quotes the following extract from the memoirs of Saint Hegesippus: 'James, the brother of the Lord succeeded to the government of the church in conjunction with the apostles. He has been called the Just by all from the time of our Saviour to the present day; for there were many that bore the name of James. He was holy from his mother's womb; and he drank no wine nor strong drink, nor did he eat flesh'.

Many Christians say to me concerning being vegan or vegetarian, "but didn't Jesus eat fish?" It's a common argument, that Jesus ate fish and would have eaten lamb at the Passover meal. This is an assumption, there is no clear evidence, though in Luke 24:43 it says the disciples gave Jesus a piece of broiled fish and some honeycomb, and he took it and ate in their presence. Did he take both, it says He took 'it': it was a 'piece' of fish, it doesn't say a whole fish. We do not know for sure, and was it taken to be polite, was it taken to prove to the disciples He was alive in flesh and bones. He showed them His hands and His feet but they still did not believe. So, Jesus said, "Have you any food here?" This suggests he took the food purely to prove he had risen and was alive. Some argue that 'fish' in the New Testament did not actually mean fish as we know it today.

Nowhere does it actually state that Jesus ate lamb at the Passover, even though he did institute the Lord's supper. When the disciples and Jesus met in the upper room, He took bread, blessed and broke it, and took the cup, gave thanks and they drank from it. It doesn't say that they ate lamb.

Whatever Jesus did or did not eat, it doesn't mean that He didn't care for animals. If he did eat fish or the Passover lamb, is this a mandate or justification for us to do the same today. One thing we do know is that today's vast animal agriculture and fishing industry looks nothing like the fishing and farming practices of first-century Palestine. Also, with the endless choice of foods available for us to eat today, is it necessary for us to kill to eat?

The accounts of the Last Supper do not mention the slaughter of a lamb. The scripture does not say that Jesus ate lamb. It just says he broke bread and drank the wine. Jesus would not need to eat the flesh of a sacrificed lamb. He was sinless and he didn't need a sacrifice to atone for His sins. He himself was about to become the final sacrifice, the lamb of God without blemish and without spot.

Some Christians would site the story of the feeding of the five thousand with the five barley loaves and two fish to justify eating fish today. Again, making a connection that Jesus must have ate fish or at least endorsed the eating of fish as being acceptable. Notice in this story the emphasis is on the bread. Jesus does not eat fish in this story, the fish is with the barley loaves that the young boy has. There is no mention of the fish in early manuscripts such as the Ebionite scriptures, only the bread loaves. The whole story is figurative of Jesus being the bread of life, he is the living bread which came down from heaven (John 6:51). He then goes on to explain the act and purpose of communion, that he who eats this bread, being His flesh, and drinks my blood, will live forever. (v 53-58)

There is some thought and writings that claim that Jesus was an Essene, or that he was connected to the Essenes. There were three Jewish sects, the Pharisees, the Sadducees, and the Essenes. They were an esoteric group, a kind of monastic community, who practised communal living, and were vegetarian. Pythagoras had links to them, and he was also vegetarian. They practised natural health and remedies, making their own medicines from plants and herbs. They understood agriculture, crops and soil similar to biodynamics used for instance in wine making today. They were into healing and astronomy. They were masters of healing through mystical experience with God, and devoted themselves to learning, writing, and practising their faith. There is a school of thought that Daniel, also a vegetarian and chief astrologer, was an Essene.

In AD 325, the Council of Nicaea, the first ecumenical council of the church, removed from the canon of gospels, the Essene Gospel of Peace, the Gospel of Thomas, the Gospel of the Holy Twelve, and other writings. Constantine the Great called this Council, which composed of three hundred bishops. Their task was to separate what they considered to be divinely inspired texts from those of questionable origin. So, it was the Roman Catholic church who created the canon of Christian scripture at the Council of Nicaea. The Council was held because of so much disagreement amongst different sects over various doctrines, one being the definition of the trinity, and how it functioned. It was here at this Council that the Nicene Creed was agreed upon, which is used in Eucharistic worship in the church down to the present day. Another Council was held in AD 381, the Council of Constantinople, when the bishops unanimously affirmed orthodox trinitarian doctrine as expressed at Nicaea. The unauthorised writings about Jesus and the apostles were called the 'Hidden Books' or the 'Apocrypha', and they were subject to imperial edicts for their destruction by fire.

These works were preserved away from the authority of the state church in remote locations in Syria and Egypt. The spiritual essence of Christianity was removed with these books to serve more earthly agendas of the emergent Holy Roman Empire.

Josephus has written a detailed account of the Essenes in *The Jewish War* (c. 75 CE), with a shorter description in *Antiquities of the Jews* (c. 94 CE), claiming first-hand knowledge, he lists the Essenes as one of the three sects of Jewish philosophy alongside the Pharisees and the Sadducees. He describes them as being pious, many of the priests were celibate, there was an absence of personal property and of money, the belief in communality, and commitment to a strict observance of the Sabbath. They seemed to have admirable aspirations towards charity and benevolence, forbidding expressions of anger, they studied the books of the elders, preserved sacred writings and lived a contemplative lifestyle. There was a community living in the Qumran area, they preserved old scrolls in a scroll jar, and it is thought that they preserved the Dead Sea Scrolls. They believed in equality and were contemptuous of wealth and so lived simple lives. It is recorded that there were 4,000 in Judea at the times of Jesus. Perhaps he was an Essene, he would certainly have known of them, though it is more likely that he merely associated with them. They were led by a council of twelve people and they were Messianic. According to the *Manual of Discipline of the Essenes*, they regularly held a ritual communion meal to bless the first fruits of the bread and wine, and believed the Messiah to be present in spirit. I don't want to give an absolute opinion either way, though I would like to think he was an Essene and that he was also vegetarian. I am sure he would be if he was living amongst us today.

There are some pointers that may suggest Jesus's link with the Essenes. The Christian Nazarene Ebionites had originated out of the Essenes, Nazareth being the home of

Jesus in northern Israel. Nazareth was very near Mount Carmel, the headquarters of the Essenes. There is evidence in some scroll fragments that James, the brother of Jesus, was an Essene. Josephus records that the Essenes were an ancient race of peoples whose origins were linked to Enoch. There are some parallels with the Christian mystics rising up today who aspire to walk with God as Enoch did. The Essenes would foretell the future, similar to prophecy and practice dream interpretation. They taught of the miraculous mysteries by the Righteous One. They trained their thoughts to be positive, they recognised the power of their thoughts and the impact they could have on their nation. During their morning communion and prayer, they would hold a positive thought for the day believing it would influence their day. By filling their mind with positive thoughts, they would eliminate any lack of balance. They believed that sleep can be a source of deep knowledge. They considered themselves to be enlightened and to possess mysteries and knowledge. They were influenced by Egyptian wisdom and thought, and revered the law of Moses. Acts 7:22 says, 'Moses was educated in all the wisdom of the Egyptians and was powerful in speech and action'.

The ethos of the Essenes was one of love and compassion for one another. They desired to harmonise with natural law, to be in harmony with nature. They sought unity with God, to carry a beautiful light, to examine themselves often, and believed that meditation would stop them straying from the path of light. These are universal truth and they were way ahead of their time. Many of these are aspirations held by the mystics of today, though the vocabulary used to convey their lifestyle may be different. Jesus himself had these qualities, compassion, love, kindness, peace and light.

As long as men massacre animals,
they will kill each other.
Indeed, he who sows the seed of
murder and pain cannot reap
Joy and love.
Pythagoras

Four

Participating in Death

The human body is not designed to eat meat. Our stomach acids struggle to cope with trying to digest meat. Eating meat is consuming death, participating in it, it is dead food. Our body becomes a graveyard for animals. Dead flesh has the lowest vibration of all foods. It putrefies in our bodies because it takes so long to digest, whereas plants absorb light and energy and is transferred into us.

The slaughter of animals is hardly a wholesome activity. It is a place of horror. I would go so far as to say it is satanic. God created and provided sufficient food for us. In Genesis 1:29-30 He said:

"I give you every seed-bearing plant on the face of the whole earth and every tree that has fruit with seed in it. They will be yours for food. And to all the beasts of the earth and all the birds of the air and all the creatures that move on the ground, everything that has the breath of life in it, I give every green plant for food."

After the Fall and the Flood, God's relationship with man changed, violence and corruption entered the earth as a result of man's sin, and the Lord was grieved that He made man: Now the earth was corrupt in God's sight and was full of violence.' (Genesis 6:11)

It is in this context, subsequent to the Fall, that the permission to kill for food in Genesis 9 should be understood. But it was reluctant permission, it was never God's original intention. Furthermore, this sufferance and tolerance of, 'eat all flesh for food' is far from unconditional or absolute. God was angry with the disobedience of the Israelites, but as it says in Numbers 14:18, 'The Lord is longsuffering and abundant in mercy, forgiving iniquity and transgression.'

I believe this concession is given in a tone of anger about man's decline from God's original intentions for him. Paul, in 2 Corinthians 3 talks about understanding scripture in letter and spirit or tone. In Genesis 6:7 God is greatly sorry that He had made man. So, Genesis 9:3 is a verse which causes much debate and question, and I think is said in the same tone or spirit as in Numbers 11 where the Lord hears the complaint of the Israelites saying, "If only we had meat to eat, we were better off in Egypt!" God's response is, so I will give them meat, and they won't eat it just for one or two days, or five or ten, or twenty days, but for a whole month, until it comes out of their ears and they are sick of it. This is because they again rejected the Lord. Egypt biblically is symbolic of sinfulness. The Israelites wished they had stayed in Egypt.

The verses following this controversial verse, Genesis 9:3, are important. God requires a reckoning from every beast and every man which suggests, 'every moving thing shall be food' in Genesis 9:3 means beast and man. Really? This sounds to me like an expression of God's anger, perhaps even said in a tone of sarcasm.

Genesis 9:4 and 5 go on to say:

But you must not eat meat that has its lifeblood still in it. And for your lifeblood I will surely demand an accounting from the hand of every beast I will require it, and from the hand of man.

When animals are slaughtered for meat their blood is drained from them, and this is not always after being stunned. Some religious and ritual methods drain the blood away in a barbaric and brutal way. There is nothing humane about the slaughter of animals. Killing by its very nature is inhumane.

35

So, these verses warn that when you kill you must remember that the life you kill is not your own, it belongs to God. As you kill what is not your own, either animal or human life, you are accountable to God for every life you kill. It is important to note that God does not give us a right to kill, he allows it under sufferance and with a grieving heart and not according to His original will and intention. God was sorry He had made man because he was corrupt, every inclination of the thoughts of his heart were evil all the time, and the earth was filled with violence. This is why he decided to wipe mankind from the face of the earth, except for Noah who was a righteous man, blameless among the people of his time, and he walked with God.

The Bible doesn't help the cause of animal rights, particularly when, after God had given us a vegetarian diet in Genesis 1, he then seems to change His mind by giving us permission to eat meat in Genesis 9, and it doesn't make the life of the vegan or vegetarian easy at all. This is the first argument that I am often charged with, that God allows us to eat meat. But it was not God's original intention, and He does caution against it by adding the condition that He demands an accounting and remember that the life you kill is not your own. Andrew Linzey in *Animal Theology* suggests that God allows the killing of animals for meat only under the conditions of necessity. I am not sure about that myself.

God's rights in creation are for us to recognise the right of animals to be themselves as God intended, to be liberated from the hand of human tyranny and to be cared for. That is His desire, that we value, respect and love them; Proverbs 12:10 says, 'A righteous man regards the life of his animal'. We share the earth with the amazing and wonderful variety of creatures that God created. He is a God of love and mercy. Galatians 5:22-23 lists the attributes of the Holy Spirit: love, joy, peace, longsuffering, kindness, goodness, faithfulness, gentleness, self-control. These are the fruits of the Holy Spirit which we should exemplify not just towards our human neighbour but towards all of God's creatures.

God may have allowed things, but not endorsed them. He is a God of love and compassion not of hatred and killing. Proverbs 15:17 says that, 'better is a dinner of herbs and vegetables where love is, than a fatted calf with hatred'. I cannot accept that a loving God would create living sentient beings with the intention that they should suffer, or that they should be mere commodities for us to use. I believe that God's original intention was for us to enjoy the animals he created, not eat them, abuse them or wear them. God's creation has a meaning and worth beyond mere human utility.

There is still a comfortable sentimental view of farming, despite common knowledge of factory farming, which puts a strain on the health or the animal. We still imagine cows grazing happily in daisied meadows, some do, but meat production is a very furtive industry. We have become desensitized, meat is nicely packaged and sanitised in our supermarkets and far removed from the horror of the slaughterhouse. There is no such thing as humane slaughter. It is a careless and violent process. Animals are often not stunned properly before slaughter, so can be fully conscious when their throat is slit. Slaughterhouses are not in our neighbourhoods are they, in fact I don't know where the nearest one would be where I live, they are always furtively hidden away from our view and our thoughts. They don't want us thinking about or questioning the meat that is on our plate, wondering how it got there. Chickens are dragged through electrified water shackled upside down struggling to get free and the mechanical blades often miss their throat and slash other parts of the body.

Current dairy farming methods mean that thousands of dairy cows will spend most of their lives indoors in cattle cubicles, restricting their movement, not allowing them the opportunity to exercise, groom and scratch themselves nor forage. They will be intensively farmed, which means they will produce a calf every year for four years after which time they will be exhausted and culled, having been milked to death. A cow has a natural lifespan of twenty years. What will happen to the calf, who knows? The female calf may join the dairy herd and if it is a bull calf it could be reared for beef or veal, perhaps exported to Europe, enduring a long journey including sea travel to live a miserable life in a veal crate, a small cubicle with a slatted floor. Such barbaric methods of keeping livestock have thankfully been banned in the UK, but not in Europe.

The Welsh government has so far refused to make CCTV compulsory for slaughterhouses in Wales, despite it being law in England and is being proposed for Scotland. Animal Aid have recently revealed the truth behind the closed doors of slaughterhouses. They captured footage of incompetence and chaos at a slaughterhouse in North Wales, witnessing a worker fail to properly stun a sheep, sheep being kneed, slapped, picked up and thrown onto the conveyor and other cruelties. They also report the very fast pace at which sheep are 'processed', with an animal being stunned on average every ten to twelve seconds. This is a small step towards improvement for the welfare of animals in slaughterhouses, as long as footage is regularly monitored by official vets, but abattoirs remain places of horror and brutality despite this legislation being implemented. The Association of Independent Meat Suppliers are not keen on the idea and have said, "The presence of CCTV will potentially make it more difficult to retain staff, and we anticipate it may be more difficult to recruit new staff to work in these areas". Why the reluctance if they have nothing to hide and welfare standards are kept? It is basically an admittance that staff do not comply and would not even apply to work in an abattoir if there were such restrictions.

Give us nothing but vegetables to eat and
water to drink. Then compare our appearance
with that of the young men who eat
the royal food.
At the end of the ten days, they looked
healthier and better nourished than any
of the young men who ate the royal food.
Daniel 1:12-15

Five

Health and Dairy

How healthy is meat-eating anyway? Our intestinal tracts are not designed to digest meat, it does not break down as easily and quickly as fruit and vegetables in the digestive system, and uses a lot of energy to do so; it then often putrefies because it takes so long. Flesh food does not supply fuel; carbohydrates provide the fuel needed for energy. Also, there is hardly any fibre content in meat, which is important for the digestive system to function healthily. Meat can also cause food poisoning, our stomach acids struggle to break it down and kill the dangerous bacteria in meat.

I would like to add a paragraph to this chapter since completing the book, about the current coronavirus pandemic. It is thought by many that there is a link between animal abuse and human health, between this virus and eating wild animals. A press release came out on 23 March 2020 stating that a leading scientist, Dr Akhtar who is a Fellow of the Oxford Animal Ethics Centre, claims that there is a direct link between human welfare and animal welfare. She reports, "Just as humans are more likely to succumb to disease when we are stressed, weakened or wounded, these same factors also suppress the immune systems in animals, leaving them extremely vulnerable to catching new infections. As a result, the worldwide animal trade creates very sick animals and ideal conditions for pathogens to multiply and jump from animal to animal, and ultimately to humans." Dr Aysha Akhtar is a neurologist and public health specialist and a Commander in the US

Public Health Service. She says that, "by creating distressed and sick animals, we are harming ourselves", and that, "three-fourths of emerging human infectious diseases come from animals. But it's not the animals' fault. If we want to prevent these diseases and save millions of people from untold suffering, we have to face the inevitable and uncomfortable truth: the real culprit is how we choose to relate with and treat animals."

So many diseases have crossed the species barrier and affected the human population. The SARS epidemic of 2003, also a coronavirus, jumped to humans from an animal called the palm civet, Spanish flu was thought to have originated in birds, and the current coronavirus is believed to have come from bats. Factory farms are ideal breeding grounds for diseases to thrive, where animals are crammed in filthy conditions that cause extreme stress. Also, we regularly feed antibiotics to farmed animals, a real recipe for disaster. Scientists have been warning us about this for years, but governments are reluctant to step in and enforce change.

Meat eating has become habit and conditioning, and some institutions promote the myth that we need meat for protein. I have never heard of anyone dying from a lack of protein, but if you are that concerned, meat is not the only source. Do we really need as much protein as we have been led to believe? Eating too much flesh protein can increase our risk of heart disease and kidney disease because the body can have trouble eliminating all the waste products of animal flesh. Protein is created in the body by amino acids which can be obtained from fruit, vegetables, nuts, seeds and bean sprouts. Some of the strongest animals on our planet, such as elephants, horses and the silverback gorilla, create protein from the grass and fruits that they eat; they do not eat flesh for strength. We can be as strong as an ox without eating beef, an ox doesn't eat meat. We do not build protein in the body from eating protein; the source of

41

protein is amino acids which are obtained from most foods that grow in the soil.

The dairy industry has fed us with propaganda, we have been brainwashed since a child into thinking that drinking milk is good for us. How can drinking the milk of another species be normal, and how can it be as healthy as they have been telling us, when it contains millions of pus cells, blood, antibiotics, bacteria, steroids and pathogens. We wouldn't want to drink human breast milk, or milk from any other animal, so why drink cow's milk, which is meant for its own baby, the calf it produces.

Daniel, in the Old Testament, resolved not to defile himself with the royal food and wine, presumably rich food which included meat. He was confident when he requested from the King that he and the three other members of the royal nobility only eat vegetables for food and water to drink, and assured the King that they would look and be healthier at the end of ten days on a plant-based diet. Daniel 1:15 records that at the end of the ten days they did look healthier and better nourished than any of the young men who ate the royal food. I know many vegan and vegetarian people who look healthy and younger than their actual age, with a wholesome look in their appearance and sparkle in their eyes. Their conscience is clear and I know myself that since eating vegan food, without being sanctimonious, I have experienced the feeling of having a clear conscience.

I am not advocating that we all become vegetarian overnight because that is not realistic, but thankfully there is an increase of interest in vegetarian and vegan food. Being vegetarian does bring with it a wholesome and healthier way of life. Flesh taints our meals, disguise it as we may; and it doesn't mean an absence of meat or protein on the plate, it means a presence of so many tasty alternatives.

People are becoming more aware that milk is not necessarily the 'health' food that we previously thought.

Whole cow's milk contains nutrients such as protein, calcium, zinc, vitamins and potassium. Calcium is considered good for bones but calcium and potassium can be obtained from many other sources, for example green leafy vegetables, soy beans, tempeh, nuts, pulses and seeds are a few. As a point of interest, the Harvard Nurses' Health Study in 2003 looked at the previously assumed link between calcium intake and osteoporosis in post-menopausal women. It demonstrated that high calcium intake was of less importance and little value than adequate vitamin D. Vitamin D can also be obtained from exposure to the sun.

Opinion is divided on whether all of the inherent nutrients remain in fat reduced milk. Milk sugar remains high in milk and many people suffer from lactose intolerance. In pasteurised non-organic milk, many of the nutrients are removed in the industrial processing. Often milk is contaminated with antibiotics and other undesirable hormones and pesticides, because intensively farmed cows are more prone to disease, lameness and stress. If you are a milk drinker the organic choice would be the healthier. An eighteen-month study in the US published in 2013 shows that it contains 24% less omega-6 fats and 62% more omega-3 fats. Cattle naturally graze on grass outdoors, whereas in modern agricultural systems dairy cattle are housed indoors on concrete floors feeding on refined grains. The exception is seen in organic farming. Milk from cows raised primarily on pasture is higher in nutrients and the healthy fat omega-3, so organic pasteurized milk is better than the conventional. An even better choice if you can get it is organic raw milk. This does have benefits, for example it is loaded with healthy bacteria, full of digestive enzymes, is rich in CLA (conjugated linoleic acid), vitamins A, B, C, D, E and K, a balanced blend of minerals and is much more digestible. When milk is pasteurized fats are oxidized and most enzymes completely destroyed. It becomes dead milk!

Milk has also been linked to breast cancer and ovarian cancer. Much research data is available on this link. A Swedish Mammography Cohort study carried out in 2004 shows evidence that high intakes of lactose and dairy products, especially milk, which contains oestrogen, may increase the risk of serious ovarian cancer and breast cancer. This could explain Japan's low rates of breast cancer, they prefer soya milk. Diets high in saturated fat and cholesterol increase the risk of heart disease.

There has been aggressive marketing of milk and dairy products which has caused confusion for some people. The dairy industry is not the wholesome industry that we imagine, where the animals are treated with care and compassion. The image of dairy cows grazing in green pastures perpetuate this notion that it is a natural and healthy product and that dairy cows do not suffer in any way to produce dairy products. I believe that the milk produced by a lactating cow is for the calf. The dairy industry is far more inhumane than people realise: female cows are artificially inseminated shortly after their first birthdays, and after giving birth they are made pregnant again by insemination, and this is a constant cycle for the life of the cow until it is exhausted and has to be slaughtered. This kind of intensive farming puts a huge strain on the cow, causing them to suffer from infections causing mastitis and lameness which cuts their life short: the average lifespan for a dairy cow is only five years. The calf is taken away from its mother when they are just one day old, and fed milk replacers so that their mothers' milk can be sold to humans. The mother is then milked three times a day, those who don't walk willingly to be milked are often beaten and abused on some dairy farms.

These days there are so many plant-based alternatives to dairy milk on the market, I drink soya, hazelnut and almond milk and have done for many years. As a teenager and during my twenties I consumed a huge amount of milk. I had ovarian cancer fourteen years ago and believe long term dairy consumption had a negative effect on my body.

Environmental issues also abound. Intensive dairy farming has a negative impact on the environment and causes an ecological burden. It contributes to greenhouse gas emissions, environmental acidification, minerals leak into ground water; slurry spreading and disposal of waste water is a problem as well as pest control. Most intensive farms are merely concerned with production yield and profit and the animals are commodities, milking machines. Organic dairy farming is much more sustainable and is based on certain principles: the health of soil, plant and animal; working with ecological systems and cycles; fairness with regard to the common environment and life opportunities. Organic agriculture involves a duty of care and is managed in a responsible manner to protect the health and wellbeing of future generations.

Humane or not, dairy products do not provide essential or beneficial nutrition for our bodies, contrary to the myth that has been perpetuated by the Milk Marketing Board that it is necessary for our health. Why are so many people suffering from lactose intolerance? Most of the world's population is genetically unable to properly digest milk and other dairy products because of lactose intolerance. We have been conditioned to believe that we need milk for calcium, and that calcium prevents one from breaking bones. This is not entirely true, and furthermore calcium is in dark leafy vegetables, sesame tahini, sea vegetables, seeds, beans and lentils, almonds, tofu to name a few. I have been drinking soya milk and other milk substitutes for the past twenty years, and have had no problems at all with my bone density. The way to have healthy bones is to get plenty of regular exercise. Dairy milk also contributes to sinus problems, all kinds of ear, nose and throat problems due to an increase in mucus formation caused by milk. It also causes acne, chronic constipation and anaemia in children. Milk thickens saliva, causing mucus and phlegm to coat the throat. Plant based milk is made for humans, dairy milk is meant for the calf.

People are drinking less and less milk and there is a decline in dairy farming. Dairy farmers in Britain suffered a fifty percent reduction in their profits in one year as the demand for cow's milk steadily declines. The Agriculture and Horticulture Development Board reported that since February 2019, thirty-five dairy farmers have left the industry with only around 8,800 dairy producers left in Great Britain and there is an ongoing decline in milking herds. This decrease in preference for cow's milk is happening worldwide. Plant based milk is the choice for twenty five percent of Britons now, and in 2018 there was a sales surge of seventy percent for oat milk and a falling demand for cow's milk.

Until we extend our circle of compassion
to all living things,
humanity will not find peace.
Albert Schweitzer

Six

Something Fishy

Many people who convert to vegetarianism find fish the most difficult food to give up. I have friends who claim to be vegetarian, but eat fish. Why are we reluctant to stop eating fish? I think the main reason is that we do not believe, or cannot conceive, the fact that they may feel pain. Also, they are out of sight underneath water, either in rivers, the ocean, or well-hidden in fish farms, so we do not relate to them in any way. Unless we fish as a hobby, sport or as our job, many of us will rarely see fish, other than in the fishmongers, unlike farm animals which we see in fields all around us. Perhaps we are in denial about any pain or suffering endured by fish because of their size, in the same way that we think about chicken. We are less disturbed at the thought, if we do think about, the killing of a fish compared to the brutality involved in slaughtering a cow. Also, our collective conscience tells us that fish is healthy.

Because of the overfishing of wild fish, the number of fish farms has greatly increased. Another word adopted for this practice is aquaculture. In other words, fish crammed together like sardines in a tin in floating cages in marine environments and underwater habitats, either in seawater or freshwater. As in all farming in large quantities, it is an unhealthy way to breed, rear and produce food. The nature of factory farming attracts problems that have to be controlled, usually with lots of chemicals. They are unnatural environments to raise fish and they are rife with diseases, pollutants and parasites, such as sea lice, that have to be treated with antibiotics and pesticides. The fish are usually housed in crowded and cramped conditions. High densities of fish result in a significant amount of pollution from fish excrement and uneaten food, which creates poor water quality high in ammonia and low in oxygen.

Salmon are meant to spend most of their lives swimming freely in the oceans and can live for sixteen years, whereas they spend one to two years in these underwater net or cage prisons before they are killed. Up to 50,000 are confined in each sea cage. They are packed so tightly together that their behaviour is unnatural, swimming incessantly in circles around the cage. The stress these crowded conditions cause makes them prone to disease, and intensively farmed salmon are prone to eye problems, such as cataracts. According to a report by Compassion in World Farming submitted to the Government, tightly stocked fish are prone to fin and tail injuries, blinding cataracts, disease outbreaks, serious infestation of salmon by sea lice and high rates of mortality. Sea lice is a serious welfare problem that can cause death in salmon due to the lice feeding off the head of the salmon until its skull can become exposed.

Hydrogen peroxide has been used on some farms to bathe the fish which can cause some to die. Also, wrasse, small fish used to feed on parasites are used, they are called cleaner fish. But often the wrasse are eaten by larger salmon or die from the stress of transport to the farm.

Genetic engineering has been used to manipulate the fish so that they become fish machines. Tampering with nature in this way causes more suffering for the fish, increasing their stress levels, and can cause them to have breathing problems and other welfare issues. Furthermore, it is unknown as yet what effects genetically modified salmon will have on humans. They are given a growth hormone, and way more growth hormones than normal. According to GM Watch, GM salmon is potentially dangerous to your health. It is known that the hormones put in beef, create a hormone called IGF, which increases insulin formation. Higher levels of IGF lead to higher levels of cancer. It also reports that fishing communities on the west coast and in Alaska are very opposed to GM salmon, and farmed salmon in general, because of the damage they could cause in the wild salmon fisheries that they depend on for their livelihood.

Slaughter methods are inhumane, the fish are starved for days before killing to empty their gut. Fish are then suffocated in air or on ice, which prolongs the time it takes for the fish to become unconscious, roughly fifteen minutes. Another method used is carbon dioxide stunning in a bath of carbon dioxide saturated water, causing the fish to thrash around, they will stop moving after thirty seconds, but do not lose consciousness for four to nine minutes, so they can be still conscious while their gills are cut and allowed to bleed to death.

Fish farms also attract predators, such as seals, mink, otters and fish-eating birds which are often shot. Fish can escape from these fish farms and breed with wild fish, and genetic mixing reduces their ability to cope and survive.

Climate change is impacting aquaculture because of ocean acidification and algal blooms. Norway suffered from its worst algal bloom this year which killed around eight million salmon. Chile also suffered from algal blooms in 2016 that killed almost twenty-seven million fish. There is excessively high usage of antibiotics and other drugs in fish farms. This industry is becoming less and less sustainable. It is causing pollution from effluent and waste, the escape of millions of fish that mix with native populations and an ongoing war against fish diseases and sea lice.

Obviously, land-based aquaculture has less of an impact on local ecosystems. No doubt the industry is attempting to improve its technological development, and find proven solutions and practices to meet economic and ecological challenges. But whether the welfare of the fish can be improved in intensive farming is a question which I doubt can be solved.

Bearing in mind the suffering and stress manifested in fish raised on these intensive farms and the thrashing around when bathed in carbon dioxide, do you not think that fish do feel pain? It is clear to me that they do. For those who are doubtful, it was scientifically proven in 2003 and 2004 that fish are sentient. They may not audibly scream, but their behaviour shows evidence of their suffering, if you are willing to look. Numerous studies have been carried out which have demonstrated that fish feel and react to pain. The first conclusive evidence of pain perception in fish was found by UK scientists. This was reported by the BBC News on 30 April 2003. It was carried out at Roslin Institute and the University of Edinburgh. Marked reactions were shown, by the rainbow trout used, when exposed to harmful substances. The researcher who carried out the research, Dr Lynne Sneddon, said, "We found fifty-eight receptors located on the face and head of the trout that responded to at least one of the stimuli. Of these, twenty could be classified as nociceptors in that they responded to mechanical pressure. Eighteen receptors also responded to chemical stimulation and can be defined as polymodal nociceptors. The mere presence of nociception in an animal is not enough to prove that it feels pain, because its reaction may be a reflex.

So, the researchers injected bee venom or acetic acid into the lips of some of the trout. "Fish demonstrated a 'rocking' motion, strikingly similar to the kind of motion seen in stressed higher vertebrates like mammals. The trout injected with the acid were also observed to rub their lips onto the gravel in their tank and on the tank walls. These do not appear to be reflex responses." The fish injected with venom and acid also took almost three times longer to resume feeding than the rest of the fish.

There is ruthless wastage of non-targeted fish when using nets, crabs, starfish, sharks, young cod, and other unwanted sea creatures are dumped back into the ocean dead. The seas are being mindlessly exploited and destroyed by man, and that is without mentioning the rubbish and plastic being dumped into the oceans.

As in all intensive farming animals, fish, and birds are denied their natural habitat and their instinctive behaviour is restricted. Salmon can travel 10,000 miles in the Pacific Ocean before they return to spawn. They are amazing fish; God's creation never ceases to amaze me with the unique attributes that He has endowed on them. For example, salmon can live in salt water and fresh water. They hatch in fresh water streams and live there for a few years before venturing out to the ocean. Their bodies undergo metamorphosis to adapt to salt water. They may stay in the ocean for up to ten years before returning to spawn. They then undergo another transformation in appearance and colour, they swim upstream and are capable of leaping out of the water as they make their way back to where they were born.

In a salmon farm the fish will live a short life and be fed with fishmeal pellets as well as huge doses of antibiotics. They will have to swim around in circles, if they can, amongst the crowded cages swimming in their own faeces, pesticides, parasites, pellets of crushed fish, chemicals and dyes. Salmon are not naturally pink or red, they are an unappetising grey. They are dyed with a synthetic chemical (E161g) made from petro-chemicals which is added to their food. Wild salmon would obtain their pink colouring from eating crustaceans and shrimp.

I am not sure that people will ever completely abandon eating fish, but I think there is a need to cut back on the quantity of fish eaten, because clearly there are problems in the fishing industry that cannot be resolved as long as there is such a high demand for fish. We do overfish and this does affect the ecosystem, for example the Alaskan Stellar sea lion population is down by eighty percent because of overfishing of mackerel and cod. If too many plant-eating fish are taken from a coral reef ecosystem, algae will grow, destroying other fish and preventing light, and so the reefs die. It is ironic that wild-caught fish is being used to feed farmed fish and that is causing real problems. The fish farming industry is one of the fastest-growing food production sectors, but so much of sustainability problems have been highlighted by the media in recent years, and one wonders how much longer can it survive.

God's creation has
a meaning and worth
beyond mere
human utility.

Seven

Animal Experiments

Another abuse of animals is their use in experiments to test cosmetics and for medical research. Such a primitive act cannot be justified in a civilised world, particularly as there are more accurate alternative methods which can be and are being used, but cost more, such as cell, tissue and organ culture. Cells from any organ of the human body can be grown in culture and also small pieces from whole organs can be cultured, which exactly represents the metabolism of an organ. Animal experiments are not a reliable way to test products, as has been shown in the past, but still the lesson has not been learnt, a multitude of drugs passed as safe on animals have since caused serious often deadly side effects in humans – Opren, Eraldin, Osmosin and Flosint for example. Species differences is not taken into account. Even Florey, who purified penicillin, admitted that it was a 'lucky chance' that he had not tested it on guinea pigs, because it kills them.

Whether animal experiments are accurate and are helpful to the health and longevity of humankind, or not, I think we are overlooking the question of whether it is right or wrong to use animals for our own ends, and in this cruel way. Animals do not exist to serve us, and they are certainly not meant to be laboratory tools or things for us to use as a means to human ends. Is it morally acceptable to deliberately breed animals for us to inflict suffering on them in the hope that they may bring a cure for our own, sometimes self-inflicted, illness and diseases? I must add here that our health issues are certainly not always self-inflicted, but many are due to diet and lifestyle. I also realise that discussing this issue of animal experimentation invites criticism of insensitivity to human sickness and the suffering of man. This leads to the question, is the suffering of animals valid if it aids humankind? This is a moral dilemma, and one would have to draw their own conclusion. The verse in Genesis 1 which talks about dominion over all creatures does not help, particularly as some people interpret this verse as literally having dominion and rule over every other creature that is not human, and they see animals as subordinate to us and at our mercy. Added to this is Genesis 9 where Noah is told that, 'the fear and dread of you will fall upon all the beasts of the earth and all the birds of the air, upon every creature that moves along the ground, and upon all the fish of the sea; they are given into your hands'. No wonder many animal lovers and animal rights activists and campaigners are not interested in Christianity, and are very much against it, because they see it as having contributed towards cruelty to animals for centuries. As I have mentioned elsewhere, dominion means unselfish guardianship and compassion towards all creatures. My own view is that animal testing is morally unacceptable and we should bring an end to all institutionalised animal experimentation.

We have not moved on from the days of the seventeenth century when the French philosopher, and supposed Christian, Rene Descartes, claimed that animals were automata, in other words nothing more than insentient machines, like clocks. He was also the man who went to great lengths in his *Discourse on Method and the Meditations* to explain and prove the existence of God. Firstly, he established the belief that he is a thing whose essence it is to think and which he claims to conceive with, 'clear and distinct perception'. (Rene Descartes, Discourse on Method and the Meditations (Penguin Books, London, 1968, p.113)). So, the ability to think is the whole essence of Descartes' being and the substance of his existence. He moves on from this theory to assert, "I conclude so evidently that God exists", because it is a clear and distinct idea in the mind. As the clear and distinct awareness of Descartes' own thought proved to him his own existence, the knowledge of God clearly and distinctly comprehended as an idea in his mind leads him to believe that God does exist. However, this is mind knowledge, there is no mention of the heart; feelings and the senses, he claimed, are unreliable. He certainly had no feelings of compassion towards animals, presumably because they had no capacity in his mind to think, so therefore he deduced they did not exist! He clearly regarded them as inferior beings because he considered the mind the superior faculty and quite frankly viewed God's creation with contempt.

There was a time when black people were considered unequal to the rest of the human race, so much so that their only usefulness was that of being slaves, until William Wilberforce, also a founder of the RSPCA, led the fight against Negro slavery in the British Empire. Henry Salt points out, in his book, *Animals' Rights*, "The present condition of the more highly organised domestic animals is in many ways very analogous to that of the Negro slaves of a hundred years ago: look back, and you will find in their case precisely the same exclusion from the common pale of humanity; the same hypocritical fallacies, to justify that exclusion; and as a consequence, the same deliberate stubborn denial of their social 'rights'". (p.21)

The subject of animal experimentation is an area which I find most distasteful and hideous, to think that this barbaric practice still persists in this day and age. According to Animal Aid:

Each year inside British laboratories, around four million animals are experimented on. Every eight seconds, one animal dies. Cats, dogs, rats, mice, guinea pigs, rabbits, monkeys and other animals are used to test new products, to study human disease and in the development of new drugs. They are even used in warfare experiments. Animal Aid opposes animal experiments on both moral and scientific grounds. Animals are not laboratory tools. They are sentient creatures capable of experiencing pain, fear, loneliness, frustration and sadness. To imprison animals and deny them their freedom to express natural instincts and to deliberately inflict physical pain in the name of science is unacceptable. All the more so because the experiments are bad science in the first place: they do not produce information that can be reliably applied to people. Ending animal experiments will benefit people as well as animals. The many differences – both obvious and very subtle – between humans and other species make animal experiments a waste of time, effort, money and lives, both human and animal.

Animal experimentation is mostly carried out because of the pathogens and toxins in products which we use and consume. The addition of pathogens and toxins in our cosmetics, toiletries, household cleaning agents is not necessary. Chemicals are harmful to us anyway, whether tested on animals or not. There are plenty of alternative cosmetics, toiletries and cleaning agents available which do not contain harmful and unnecessary additives which are perfectly effective and actually much more pleasant to use. They do not contain those dreadful strong-smelling chemicals which you know are harmful.

Thankfully, some progress has been made in the field of cosmetic testing, but still there are countries, such as China, who are demanding that cosmetics be tested on animals. The obvious way that we can help is to make cruelty-free choices and there are plenty of products available, now more than ever.

There are more reliable methods of testing, and have been for years, that are non-animal methods. Testing on animals for the toxicity of cosmetics, cleaning agents or medicines, has never been reliable. Toxins and chemicals that humans may be affected detrimentally by do not necessarily affect animals, and vice versa. Animals should not be used as commodities in this way, it is cruel and it is immoral.

The Hadwen Trust, renamed in 2017, 'Animal Free Research UK', has existed for over forty years. Their vision is to create a world where human diseases are cured faster without animal suffering. There are various and more advanced ways of testing substances and researching for disease. Stem cells can replicate such cells as brain or muscle cells. Organs on a chip are the next exciting development in 3D cell culture. They are organs which are made up of real, living human cells which mimic a real organ. Drugs can be designed by computer, tested for toxic effects in human cells, and its pharmacology studied in the whole human by sophisticated separation and analytical techniques.

Animal experimentation is stopping medical progress because information from animal research cannot be applied to humans. Not only is it unethical, but it is unreliable because animals' bodies are different to ours. Substances which may harm us may not harm animals. So many mistakes have been made in the past, the thalidomide debacle being one that stands out in history.

Another dark and troubling practice is the use of animals in warfare experiments. These include blast injury research, the testing of chemical and biological agents such as nerve gases. Porton Down is one of the main organisations that use animals in their development of countermeasures to the constantly evolving threat posed by chemical and biological weapons. Animals are obviously exposed to poisonous substances which cause horrific suffering and deaths of thousands of animals. An Early Day Motion was tabled in February 2019 in Parliament which states:

That this House notes with concern that, each year, thousands of animals of various species including monkeys, mice, pigs and guinea pigs, are experimented upon using chemical, biological and other weapons, causing prolonged and extensive suffering; notes that, whilst these experiments are not conducted to develop or test offensive weapons, that the animal's suffering can continue for hours until the animal dies, or is killed, and that an example of the symptoms from exposure to such weapons has included writhing, substantial incapacitation, no meaningful voluntary movement, gasping, continuous tremor, production of tears and visible production of saliva; further notes that the suffering so endured is in addition to the standard deprivations of life in a laboratory, restriction on movement, inability to choose cage-mates, inescapable stressors, such as human presence, light and sound; further notes that, in 2017 alone, at Porton Down, 3,865 animals were experimented upon for purposes including medical countermeasures to biological and chemical agents, the detection and identification of biological agents; and calls on the Government to introduce a ban on the use of living animals for warfare experiments. (EDM 2113)

The excitement they experience
when they murder an unarmed
animal is entirely due
to their deep feelings
of inadequacy and impotence
in ordinary life.
John Cleese

Eight

Animal Sports/Hunting

There are three motives behind blood sports and hunting. Firstly, there are such sports as fox hunting and trophy hunting which are cruel and pursued for the insane so-called pleasure of humans. Secondly, there is the killing such as pheasant shooting for fun and food. Thirdly, there are those who consider certain animals to be vermin, pests or a mere nuisance in their anthropocentric world. These types of humans consider it their responsibility to maintain a balance in nature by determining what should live and what shall die. They don't look around and realise what a mess they are making, they are working against nature rather than with it. They underestimate the power of nature which will rebel and make itself heard regardless of man's attempts to subdue it. Man cannot dominate and repress nature, we are part of it, we should be living in harmony with nature. Thankfully, young people today know this and they are leading the way, they are standing up and will not give in until action is taken to restore and improve our environmental problems. This has never happened on such a scale before.

What right does man have to select and kill certain birds because we don't like their habits, demonise certain animals and call them vermin and try to annihilate them. What sense is there in racing dogs to chase hares for entertainment. Frankly, I don't see the point in horse racing or any other animal racing for a bet. If a species does not fall in with our interests as humans they will be exterminated. Why would anyone with any compassion want to go to a bull fight, another cruel sport used for sadistic entertainment. It has nothing to do with tradition, it is all about pure unadulterated torture. It is an absolute disgrace and a mortal sin.

I don't think God created animals for any entertainment that involves unnatural behaviour and humiliation, where wild animals such as elephants and tigers are condemned to a lifetime of confinement in a cage unable to express normal behaviour. Thankfully, in May 2019, the Environment Secretary, Michael Gove, introduced a new legislation to ban the use of wild animals in travelling circuses.

There is more to fox hunting than many people realise. The fox is seen as a pest by the hunting fraternity, and most hunt supporters will insist that it is necessary to protect poultry and livestock. Foxhunting is not a humane way to kill a fox, the purpose is prolonged pleasure. The hounds are bred for stamina not speed so that they can run for hours until the fox is exhausted.

The Hunting Act banned hunting foxes with dogs in 2003, but statistics show that it has not been implemented. Hunts find loopholes and some continue with their sport regardless, some continue hunting under the guise of trail hunting.

There are sinister aspects to this bloodthirsty sport, one is cub hunting, and the other is terrier work. The cub hunting season starts in August and is usually carried out as early as six in the morning in the heart of the countryside well away from the public eye. It is the practice of training young hounds by killing fox cubs. A covert is surrounded and hounds sent in mercilessly. Terrier men are usually involved, they are the thugs who use terriers to flush out and ensure a killing. As a past hunt saboteur myself, I know how threatening and menacing the terrier men are to protestors, they are a rough bunch. If the fox or cubs go down an underground sanctuary, the terrier men will dig out and send their dog down. Basically, it turns into a dog fight underground but the terrier men will ensure the fox is killed with a gun if necessary. Sometimes they will pull the fox out by the tail and throw it to the hounds who will tear it to pieces, club it to death or put it in a sack to be released some distance away for further hunting fun.

Closely linked to fox hunting and those involved is pheasant and partridge shooting. Many of us have seen beautiful colourful pheasants on the roadside and in fields in the countryside, and no doubt many of them are shot for sport amongst the rich and well connected. But these game birds are also bred and mass-produced in cages, hatcheries and pens so that they can be shot by wealthy landowners and their cronies for fun. They will pay at least £1,000 a day for the 'privilege' to shoot grouse, this is how the wealthiest and influential people in the land spend their leisure time. The season of shooting begins on 12 August and ends on 10 December, it is known as the Glorious Twelfth! Any birds of prey or any indigenous mammals that are a threat to their interest, such as foxes, stoats, hen harriers and buzzards are either trapped in snares, shot or illegally poisoned by the gamekeeper. He will justify his activity by labelling the victims as vermin and pests. All of this to provide entertainment for the elite minority!

It seems that farmers, fox hunters, grouse shooters, gamekeepers and so on do not necessarily care about conservation or good management of land as they claim to do so. They are mainly interested in their fun days out running around the countryside on horseback to kill foxes, which they see as vermin, or their country sport of shooting grouse and pheasants, and killing any other animal or bird that gets in the way of their sport. Any wildlife seen as a threat to the birds is slaughtered. How is that conservation?

The grouse moors where the shoots happen are being destroyed by burning of the moorland to create heather as food and shelter for the intended quarry. This damages

64

delicate eco-systems and degrades the carbon-rich peat which affects drainage and is a contributing factor in the cause of flooding in moorland areas. Ditches are also dug out to drain water to encourage the growth of heather, and the ground loses its ability to soak up rain and runs off into the villages and towns. The Walshaw Moor has been ploughed in parallel lines approximately ten metres apart, running from high to lower ground. At various junctures, they drain into nearby watercourses. Hebden Bridge which lies beneath the Moor, is an example of an area that has suffered catastrophic flooding in recent years, which has been attributed to burning on the moors, general mismanagement, building of car parks and roads, and drainage of wet areas to encourage heather growth on the grouse moors.

The irony is that this destruction of land is rewarded with public money, their activities are subsidised through what is known as the Single Payment Scheme and the Environmental Stewardship programme. Roughly £20m is paid out in England alone. So, farmers are getting these subsidies to supposedly manage the land, but actually they are using it for their own hedonistic ends. Single Farm Payments are distributed under the Common Agricultural Policy to more than 100,000 farmers. The owner of Walshaw Moor at Hebden Bridge received £250,000 a year which is double his reported annual running costs. Many of these moors are owned by tycoons who are well connected with government officials and agents, and they will claim that they are environmentally conscientious in order to receive subsidies. A written letter or word of mouth reassurance from the land owner is often sufficient. Under the Environmental Stewardship programme, moor estate owners can claim for maintenance, restoration and projects that are conducive to good environmental practices. The money is tied to government-approved management plans, and burning and herbicide use is included, hardly beneficial to the environment.

Participants in the sport of grouse shooting will be a network of old boys and well-connected decision makers such as investment bankers, stockbrokers, landowners and members of the peerage and some members of the royal family. Those involved in grouse shooting will claim that they are managing the countryside and the natural environment on our behalf. They purport to be responsible and respected members of society who are controlling what they perceive to be pests and vermin and they are having a jolly day out in the process.

Another so called fun pursuit is trophy hunting. A trophy hunting website describes their ethos, "It is about ethical hunting … it's about quality trophies … it's about a memorable African Safari, but it's also about family! A family business based on solid family values, offers you all this in a setting that is a home away from home".

The 'big five', the lion, buffalo, elephant, leopard and rhino, are a pleasure to hunt, it boasts! There is also common game species in abundance on the farm: baboon, wildebeest, eland, gemsbok, giraffe, impala, kudu, lynx, ostrich, steenbuck, velvet monkey, warthog, waterbuck, buffalo, zebra, sable, hyena, porcupines, and mountain reedbuck. And this is just one safari farm, with no value placed on the life of these amazing animals, other than to make a buck for the owner, and for pleasure, leisure and fun for those who visit these safari farms.

The Safari Club blatantly claim to practice ethical hunting, how can hunting be ethical? They assert that they give back by participating in conservation (another dichotomy). How can killing be conserving? They add that they 'participate in humanitarian efforts taking place around the globe', to justify their brutal pastime.

I cannot see where and how conservation is a justification for hunting wild animals. Conserving what?

The only purpose in this field of sport is the conservation of the animals in the safari park for hunters to kill. Nothing ethical about that! The Safari Club are constantly clutching at moral straws to justify their blood sport. A book was written in 1995 by James A. Swan entitled *A Defense of Hunting*. He argues it is a spiritual ritual, a meaningful act sparked by a spiritual love for nature, hunting is a spiritual act of love. He claims a hunter is deeply in touch and in love with nature, even the moon favours them. He mentions the hunter's moon a lot, and the magic and mystery of hunting. Apparently, the hunt can be a great teacher of much more than the techniques of killing, it can be the keys to happiness, health and peace. How can one have peace and a clear conscience after killing an animal to show it off as a trophy, to boost their ego and manhood, and to express their repressed anger?

Furthermore, there are awards and medals to be attained from the achievement of Safari Club members who regard it as a privilege to 'harvest' these animals. Somehow, it is seen as contributing to wildlife despite the fact they are taking away from what has been created. They are taking what is not their own. In Psalm 50 the Mighty One declares,

"For every beast of the forest is Mine,
And the cattle on a thousand hills.
I know all the birds of the mountains,
And the wild beasts of the field are Mine".
When God said in Genesis 1:26,
"Let us make man in our image, in our likeness, and let them rule over the fish of the sea and the birds of the air, over the livestock, over all the earth, and over all the creatures that move along the ground",

He didn't say, 'fill the earth' by breeding wild animals, 'subdue it and rule over it' (Genesis 1:28) by killing them for a fun way to spend their yearly holiday/vacation, and to increase their collection of African big five or other trophies to act out their internalised anger and sadistic tendencies. These verses in Genesis, I would interpret as compassionate and responsible care for God's creation. Contrary to the claims of hunters that it is a humane activity, it is nothing less than brutal and savage. They not only use various types of guns but also bows and they prolong the suffering of the victim.

There can be no valid justification for the activities of trophy hunters and the Safari Club. Killing animals to use them as trophies and using the revenue, as they claim they do, to fund conservation, is not acceptable. The UK government are currently having a consultation with a view to banning the import of these so-called trophies. Zac Goldsmith MP has campaigned for many years against trophy hunting, which sees hunters pay huge fees to kill threatened wild animals, like lions, elephants and rhinos. He has said that it is morally indefensible and that a higher value should be placed on animals alive rather than dead.

I think Matthew Scully sums this sport up well in his excellent book entitled *Dominion*, on the power of man, the suffering of animals, and the call to mercy. He says that hunters are, 're-creating creatures for recreation'. We as Christians, are carriers of light! Should we be participating in such barbaric and cruel sports that involve the killing of God's creatures for pleasure or any other reason? Without naming names, I know this is a common practice in the US, even in Christian circles.

Many people consider horse racing to be a harmless sport, and that the horses are willing participants and enjoying the race. But they tend to overlook the fact that there is a dark side to this so-called sport of kings, and in this country, it is one of the Queen's favourite sports. There usually is a furtive side when there is profit and amusement for the benefit of man involved. It is estimated that there are two hundred thoroughbred deaths each year, and they are cruel deaths which happen on the racecourse during a race.

The Grand National is a notoriously hazardous race. Jump racing causes the most fatalities. The horses are bred and trained for speed, which makes them vulnerable to injury, and worse. Typically race horses die, or are killed, as a result of a broken limb or neck, spinal injuries or a heart attack, and of course these deaths will rarely be reported in the media. When they are no longer financially viable, they are usually slaughtered.

Approximately 13,000 foals are born each year for the British and Irish racing industries, and not all of them will be suitable for racing and evidence suggests, because they are not always accounted for, that the 'failures' will be killed, fed to hunting hounds or butchered for meat. It is assumed that racehorses are well looked after, some may well be, but they will be confined to stables for much of their day, and when they are no longer profitable or useful, they will be taken to the abattoir. The racing industry will, of course, say that fatalities and deaths are tragedies that happen, just like in motor racing or any other human sport. But the horse has no choice in whether it wants to race or not, it is forced to, it is at the mercy of the will of humans.

Whipping is another cruel aspect of horse racing, and the fact that Norway banned the use of the whip in 1982, suggests that it is a contentious issue, and there have been campaigns being run for years by the various animal charities to ban the whip from racing in Britain. It was reported in the Daily Mail on 19 December 2019, that, 'The Horse Welfare Board are set to recommend an urgent consultation on the use of the whip when it publishes its Horse Welfare Strategy in February, a document that will contain a range of options including a blanket ban'. The British Horseracing Authority stipulates that the whip is used, firstly to keep the rider safe, and secondly for 'encouragement'. A 2011 University of Sydney report, *An Investigation of Racing Performance and Whip Use by Jockeys in Thoroughbred Races,* concluded that whipping does not improve performance. The report said that, 'On average, they achieved highest speeds when there was no whip use, and the increased whip use was most frequent in fatigued horses. That increased whip use was not associated with significant maintenance of velocity as a predictor of superior race placing at the finish of the race'. Animal Aid's report on the beating of a horse during racing concludes:

A ban on the use of the whip for 'encouragement' would prevent a great deal of unjustifiable animal cruelty. Using the whip for encouragement means that animals are being beaten, before a paying public, for self-gain on the part of the jockey and his 'connections'. Race horses are the only animals who can be beaten in public in the course of a 'sporting' event. Other animals are protected from such treatment.

How many are your works, O Lord!
In wisdom you made them all;
The earth is full of your creatures.
There is the sea, vast and spacious,
teeming with creatures beyond number –
living things both large and small.
There the ships go to and fro,
and the leviathan, which you
formed to frolic there.
Psalm 104: 24-26

Nine

Senseless Sadistic Slaughter

Are there any of God's creatures exempt from exploitation for the commercial use of mankind. The Animal Rights movement has had its work cut out for decades, campaigning against the endless cruelties perpetrated on animals. The beautiful seal and majestic whale are not excluded, and I do not relish writing this chapter. In fact, I have found it painful writing much of this book. The harming of both these mammals has provoked outrage over the years, namely seal clubbing and whaling. They are being blamed for fishery declines. Baby seals are also killed for their fur. Most of the seal hunters are fishery workers. Ninety-eight percent of the seals killed during the seal hunt will be under three months of age. Most British people would abhor the idea of baby seal clubbing, though they allow the slaughter of lambs quite happily. The value of an animal seems to be dictated by the personal values, occupation, motives, circumstances of the humans or culture it lives in. One man's hobby is another man's horror.

In the nineteen eighties, there was no let-up of the outrage towards seal hunters and they were driven out of business. Sealers became stigmatised, and rightly so. But, like many cruel and unnecessary practices, if there is money and a commercial venture beckoning, the latent greed is often reignited and they re-emerge and find some false justification for their trade. According to data made available by the Canadian Government, 2,382 seals were killed in one day this year. They are killed from a helicopter with a rifle and often they are not killed by the first bullet and will die a slow death. If they are still alive, they will be hooked onto vessels and clubbed to death.

According to the Humane Society, many countries around the world have all banned the trade in seal skins and other products from seal hunts. There is no demand for seal meat or their oil. They are positive and determined to bring an end to this practice and commercial trade once and for all. They promised to the seals, years ago, that they would never stop campaigning and pressurising governments until peace had been restored to the ice floes.

The Psalmist praised God for His greatness, His majesty and the works of His hand for the sea vast and spacious, teeming with creatures beyond number, and the leviathan, which He formed to frolic there. But man has not allowed this majestic giant of the seas, the leviathan, to play and enjoy its life in the ocean. The corrupt heart of man sees this beautiful mammal as commercial gain and an object to be exploited.

Countries such as Japan are persistent in looking for loopholes to bans and finding ways to continue the trade of whaling. Greenpeace have been opposing whale hunting for years, and there has been an international dispute raging around these dignified and serene mammals who glide with beauty and grace through the seas. Yet Japan seems to defy any criticism, and after some years of respite for the whales, Japan resumed hunting whales this year. The problem is the Japanese hunters are proud of their brutal killings and see each killing as something to celebrate. They claim it has always been part of their national culture to eat whale meat. Then they changed their justification for whaling to scientific research though there hasn't been any sign of progress or scientific discovery concerning whales as a result of their practices. Now they have returned to whaling for meat consumption, even though the demand for whale meat has gone down dramatically in recent years, yet some

Japanese still see it as part of the nation's culinary culture. There is a stubbornness in that Japan makes the argument that it is their cultural right to continue whaling, even though much of the population are not keen on eating whale meat.

As in the case of the trend towards vegan and vegetarianism which is increasing worldwide, it is the younger populations who have the insight to see that it is neither sustainable, healthy or necessary. Also, in the case of whale meat, it will probably be the older generations amongst the fisheries who are digging their heels in on this subject, and I believe it will come to an end permanently within this next decade, as people worldwide are becoming more enlightened and this enlightenment is spreading and pervading every aspect of our lives rapidly. I do believe that this is an aspect and a sign of the establishment of God's Kingdom on earth as it is in Heaven. This is why I am confident in my belief that we are rapidly returning to the peaceable kingdom, to an Eden-like state.

Japan are no longer members of the International Whaling Commission, so they tend to do their own thing though it is often amidst confrontations with Greenpeace's ship, the Sea Shepherd, the marine conservation group which has tirelessly fought against atrocities such as whaling, seal clubbing and dolphin killing. Japan say they carry out whale hunts for research purposes, but they have been known to use the whales for meat. An article in the Guardian dated 1 July 2019 reports that fisheries officials are hoping that the resumption of commercial whaling will spark renewed interest in whale meat among Japanese consumers. But the International Fund for Animal Welfare said the resumption of commercial whaling will not magically increase market demand. They believe it is the beginning of the end.

The Japanese government are using tax-payers money to prop up the industry, but the appetite of the population for whale meat is waning. IFAW are calling for the development of whale watching along Japan's coastline, which will inculcate an appreciation of these gentle giants of the ocean in their natural habitat, frolicking in the sea as God intended.

To me, the thought of any animal, bird, fish or mammal being killed is disturbing and really does provoke anger which rises up inside. But the beautiful dolphin, is it included in this senseless massacre? Yes, they are, there aren't many of God's creatures that go un-tormented by man. No wonder God tells Noah that the fear and dread of man will fall upon every creature. Dolphins are hunted in Japan for meat, but also for marine park aquariums. The fisheries at Taiji claim that they need dolphin and whale meat to survive. This is not true, it is not necessary in these days of plentiful availability of nutritious plant food, it is certainly not a vital food source.

Fur looks best
on its original owner.

Ten

Fashion and Fur

In Genesis 3:21, the Lord God made garments of skin for Adam and his wife and clothed them. It is often assumed this was animal skin. Skin or leather can be made from leaves, fruit skins, coconut, grass, tree bark, to name just a few plants. Many clothing brands are currently working towards the future and coming up with innovative vegan textiles. One of the most beautiful skins used to make handbags and other accessories is currently being made from teak leaf leather.

For the past thirty odd years, since the animal rights activists of the eighties campaigned against the fur trade, it has been a taboo to buy or wear a fur coat, though it never went away completely. It has made a comeback and the battle goes on against real fur, and the fight may never go away, until the restoration of creation. If the debate on this issue becomes about biodegradability and carbon footprint, research has been done on both sides, though fake fur comes out as the most ecologically responsible choice.

With the increase of people becoming vegetarian or vegan, the awareness of animal cruelty is higher on the agenda, and those same people will not want to wear fur and would disapprove of their friends doing so, and even despise the wearing of fur.

There is no such thing as the humane production of animal fur. The PETA website informs how fur-bearing animals are electrocuted anally and genitally in order to limit damage to the fur. New York is the first state to have banned this inhumane method. They also report that, 'eighty-five percent of the fur industry's skins come from animals who were held captive on fur factory farms, where they were crammed into severely crowded, filthy wire cages. Many were later beaten or electrocuted, and sometimes even skinned alive'. Fur farming is one of the cruellest practices, hidden from human view, with no protection laws or penalties for abusing animals, and again China is the worst culprit. The fur industry causes unimaginable suffering and pain to animals, and with so many different options for warm and fashionable fabrics, it has become an unnecessary and archaic industry. Thankfully, many countries, including the UK in 2000, and many over Europe, have banned, or are phasing out, the production of fur. There is good news, in that the Queen has recently made the compassionate decision not to acquire any new fur items. PETA report that 95% of Brits refuse to wear real fur, and that now is the time to urge the government to ban the importation of fur and make the UK a fur-free nation. The campaign needs to continue, because this cruel trade is unacceptable and barbaric in the twenty first century.

It is unnatural to keep wild animals such as foxes and mink in small wire mesh cages which inherently have low welfare standards, and 85% of fur sold globally is from farming, with the remainder from trapping and hunting wild animals. Fur farming, by its very nature, is rife with welfare issues. The cramped and monotonous battery cage system causes severe welfare problems for wild animals who are deprived of their natural habitat, for example, mink need to swim and foxes express important natural behaviour through digging. Research has been done into domesticating foxes and mink but apparently this changes the quality of their fur, and even if this were possible it remains an inhumane industry, not only because wild animals are kept in cages but the methods of slaughter are brutal.

The Scientific Review of Animal Welfare Standards and 'WelFur' (2015) concluded that, 'Enrichment of existing housing systems is not sufficient to address the serious welfare problems inherent in cage systems. The use of undomesticated animals by the fur industry means that fear of humans and difficulties in handling and management would present insurmountable obstacles to the adoption of more extensive systems. It is therefore impossible for the needs of mink and foxes to be met by the fur industry. A ban is the only viable solution to the serious welfare concerns highlighted in this report'.

Some people may place a low value on foxes and mink, but to me all animals are equal and worthy of the same consideration of their welfare. Whether fur farming is environmentally friendly, sustainable or has no significant carbon footprint, to me it is still morally wrong and unnecessary, as well as being downright cruel, because it involves the use of animals for the purpose of vanity.

Thankfully, PETA have reported that, 'more so than ever before, people are against wearing animals. From mohair hats to shearling jackets to leather shoes, shoppers are ditching cruel and environmentally toxic items in favour of compassionate and sustainable vegan clothing'. PETA have been an active and radical campaigner against using animals for clothing, they have always used graphic photographs and detailed descriptions of the horrific methods used to obtain fur, leather, wool, cashmere and mohair. Their investigations of these industries have repeatedly exposed widespread abuse of animals. There have been huge advancements in textiles and earth-friendly vegan materials are indistinguishable from and far superior to their animal-derived counterparts. Recycled rubber, plastic bottles, tree bark, coconut fibre and recycled polyester and cotton blends are some examples of materials being used to produce high quality clothing, which are vegan and cruelty free and using no chemicals.

Animals are not ours to wear, and they do not belong in our wardrobes!

There is sufficiency in the world
for man's need
but not for man's greed.
Mahatma Gandhi

Eleven

Population Growth/Food Resources

What does the Lord require of you but to act justly, to love mercy, and to walk humbly with your God?
Micah 6:8
Eating animals as we do in the West leads to global poverty. Millions of people in Africa and many parts of the world are not getting enough to eat while the rest of us get more than sufficient. It is a well-known fact that the yield of plant produced per acre compared to an acre used for cows to graze is far more economical. Eighty three percent of farmland is used for animal farming, and to make this land available, ancient forests are being erased and whole habitats destroyed, and animals living in them displaced or killed. Fewer trees means that less carbon dioxide can be absorbed, and this is having a huge impact on wildlife as well as people and communities. Factory farming is not the solution either. Eighty five percent of all of the soya grown globally goes to feed farm animals. Rainforests have been chopped down to grow the soy and also to graze farm animals. A huge amount of energy is involved in the process of producing meat, not just the plant-based feed, which has to be shipped to a feed mill which has to be operated, then transported to a farm or factory farm. The farm has to be operated, the animal has to be raised, taken to the slaughterhouse, someone has to operate the slaughterhouse, then the meat has to be conveyed to its distribution centre or supermarket, all requiring fuel.

God expects us to look after this earth, to share it equally and not to abuse its resources. A booklet called Planet on a Plate produced by Viva says that, 'Livestock production represents an obscene waste of food and a betrayal of the world's poor'. High quality food such as wheat and soya, which could feed humans, is being fed to animals and largely wasted. The amount of feed consumed by the US beef herd alone would feed the entire populations of India and China.

Mahatma Gandhi was right when he said, "There is sufficiency in the world for man's need but not for man's greed". Has the West become gluttonous in its appetite for meat, factory farming being a consequence of this greed? Is it not unnatural and inhumane to cram livestock together to feed a population who eat far too much meat anyway?

Most of us abhor cruelty to animals, so why are we ostrich-like when it comes to factory farming where animals are denied their natural habitat; for example chicken, one of Britain's favourite meats, live a short life intensively farmed in windowless sheds under bright light to encourage maximum activity, feeding and drinking for nearly twenty four hours, not allowing rest: there is much evidence that sick birds are trampled to death in the crowded squalor and infections spread like wildfire, resulting in gross over-use of antibiotics. Ducks are farmed in the same way today and what is alarming about this practice is that they never see the light of day nor do they have access to water to bathe in.

Shouldn't we, as Christians, be more responsible stewards of God's creation? Aren't we being selfish and greedy, aren't we eating too much meat, couldn't we all help to curb climate change if we ate less meat? I say selfish because we are betraying the world's poor and starving. The International Food Policy Research Institute has calculated what the effect on the developing world would be if the industrial world reduced its meat consumption by half over a fifteen-year period. If we in the industrial world reduced our meat consumption by half, thirty-three million people would be saved from starvation, of whom 3.6 million would be children; and that is if we only reduced our consumption by half. The reason is that meat production in the West relies on the importation of grain and other foodstuffs from the developing world as animal feed. Wheat and soya are resources which could feed the poor, but are being fed to animals instead. So, food resources are being mismanaged and wasted on a grand scale.

Global population has grown, and despite there being an increase in people moving to a plant-based diet, there is also an increase in demand for animal-based products globally. According to the Creating a Sustainable Food Future Report, produced in July 2019, our current food system is dangerously unsustainable and accounts for thirty percent of the planet's greenhouse gases. There are two issues here which need to be tackled: malnourishment and starvation in some parts of the world, and also the problem of global warming. Some of the recommendations in this report include focussing on reducing growth in demand for food and agricultural products, increasing food production without expanding agricultural land. Land needs to be utilised for growing crops instead of grazing for farm animals, farmers need to consider growing crops instead of rearing farm animals for food.

Methods of growing crops has advanced over recent decades, with marker-assisted breeding and improvements in 'genomics' making conventional breeding not only faster but also better. Genetically modified crops still continue, despite much controversy. According to the above-named Report (p.185), 'most GM crops have been inserted into just four high-value crops: maize, soybeans, canola and cotton. GM crops overwhelmingly employ one of two basic traits. The first conveys absolute resistance to the herbicide glyphosate. Genetic modification has potential to improve crop breeding and increase yields, but it is the subject of by far the most contentious public policy debate surrounding plant breeding'. Much of the attention has focused on possible links between glyphosate and cancer, and according to this report it claims most studies have found little to no evidence of glyphosate causing cancer in humans. The Report also admitted that although the evidence as a whole does not show health effects, that does not mean glyphosate itself is harmless. The research and debate will continue on the controversies surrounding genetically modified food.

The Report does recommend a shift to healthier and more sustainable diets, and identifies reductions in consumption of ruminant meat (beef, sheep and goat) as the most promising strategy for reducing land requirements and greenhouse gas emissions, while also achieving health benefits. The Report also states that most people consume more protein than they need and that arguments that this animal-based protein is necessary for health, or efficient because of essential amino acids, are incorrect. The following is an extract:

Myth: More protein is better.

More protein is not necessarily better, unless an individual is malnourished or undernourished. Although the word 'protein' comes from the Greek *proteios*, meaning 'of prime importance', protein is no more important than the other nutrients required for good health, and many people do not need as much protein as they believe. .... A balanced plant-based diet can easily meet this need. Meanwhile, over-consumption of protein is linked to some health problems, including kidney stones and the deterioration of kidney function in patients with renal disease.

The Report recommends a new approach, in order to achieve a sustainable food future, which includes four strategies: move beyond reliance on information and education campaigns to effective marketing, engage the food industry, improve plant-based substitutes, and leverage government policies.

So far, we have mismanaged our planet earth, and much of it is motivated by wealth and greed with no sense of responsibility or care for balance and prosperity globally. We have exploited poorer countries, we have disregarded the effect that mass animal food production is having on our environment, and we have been wasteful. In the developing world there is a huge and growing waste problem. Tearfund, a Christian charity who work with Third World countries, are working on a policy called 'circular economy' to address poverty reduction, environmental sustainability and inequality. It is a new way of thinking about how we live, and industry is starting to embrace it. We currently have a linear economy which means we make a product, and when it breaks, we throw it away, being wasteful and inefficient. This new way of thinking, a circular economy, involves reusing, repairing, refurbishing, and rebuilding the products we use. It is a development model which creates jobs, improves health and reduces pollution. Countries such as Brazil, India and Kenya have adopted this model. Resources such as components for cars and machinery are shared, repaired and remanufactured. We cannot continue with our throw-away mentality. We need to be imaginative and innovative with new ways of manufacturing and recycling. We, in the west are advanced in so many ways, and we are beginning to make small changes, such as cutting back on plastic usage for packing, but in terms of re-using and refurbishing goods, we are not so keen, and we have to renew our thinking in this area.

The wolf will live with the lamb, the leopard will lie down with the goat, the calf and the lion and the yearling together; and a little child will lead them.

The cow will feed with the bear, their young will lie down together, and the lion will eat straw like the ox.

The infant will play near the hole of the cobra, and the young child put his hand into the viper's nest.

They will neither harm nor destroy on all my holy mountain, for the earth will be full of the knowledge of the Lord as the waters cover the sea.

Isaiah 11: 6-9

Twelve

The Restoration of all Things

God's amazing plan of salvation brought the promise of restoration into this fallen world, he brought hope and renewal. We can rejoice in the Lord and be joyful in God our Saviour. (Habakkuk 3:19). He is the God of joy, gladness and restoration. He is our strength. Isaiah 61 proclaims that God will bestow on us a crown of beauty instead of ashes, the oil of gladness instead of mourning, and a garment of praise instead of a spirit of despair, because the Lord takes delight in us! My heart leaps with joy as I write this verse!

I mentioned earlier about a movement of Christians that has been emerging over the past ten years or so who step into heavenly places or dimensions everyday of their lives. They are called Christian Mystics, and they are nothing new, there have always been Christian mystics who seek intimacy and union with God and who see spending time with Him as a priority of their everyday lives. They are people who earnestly seek out the mysteries and the depth of God, they are interested in the mystery of God, of His being, what God has done, and the wisdom of God. They engage in the depth of the love of God and yearn for a face-to-face encounter with Him. I have been interested in spiritual mysticism myself for the past four years, and am exploring the different aspects of mystical prayer, contemplative prayer, experiencing God, finding that place of rest in Him, practising the presence of God, and pursuing the deeper mysteries of God. It all began, for me, with a hunger and thirst for God and a boredom of what the church was offering, which was focussed on learning about God, rather than wanting to know Him. I cannot be satisfied any longer with good theology and doctrine. There are Sons of God rising up and they are on fire, they are engaging with God in the heavenly realms. The Father's heart is waking up the Bride. They want to be vessels of glory, ascending into Heaven, seeing the beauty realm of God, and decreeing and declaring they be so on earth. Their purpose is to manifest the Kingdom on earth, to partner with God in restoring all things, to change the atmosphere and environment and destroy the works of the devil.

I believe we are in transition between two ages, from the Age of Pisces which was the church age, to the Age of Aquarius which is the Kingdom Age. In this next age we will see a oneness with creation and the restoration of all things. The word restoration implies a return to something good, something that was taken away, a return to an original state. The word Eden comes to mind. God created the cosmos, he put the stars in the Heavens, and why did He do so? God is using astronomy as a clock. Job 26 tells us, 'He spreads out the northern skies over empty space; he suspends the earth over nothing'. He tells us in Job 38 that the constellations have seasons, and in Psalm 19, 'The heavens declare the glory of God; the skies proclaim the work of his hands'! Every culture has a mazzaroth, the Biblical Hebrew word which means constellations, or zodiac, that indicates times and seasons and they are all very much the same in each culture.

There are stories written in the stars, and God uses the cosmos to declare events, an example is when Jesus was born, when the star of Bethlehem shone brightly in the Heavens. Apparently, scientists and astronomers believe that the star was not a star at all, that it was a conjunction of planets, and it certainly was not a myth. It was something known as a triple conjunction between Jupiter and Venus, with the two planets coming close together in the sky three times over a short period. Venus is the morning star, and Jupiter is known as the King star. What is more remarkable is that this happened within the constellation of Leo, symbolising the lion of the tribe of Judah, and a full moon appeared at the same time. We are warned, in Deuteronomy 4:19, against astrology, in other words the worship of the stars, 'And when you look up to the sky and see the sun, the moon and the stars – all the heavenly array – do not be enticed into bowing down to them and worshiping things the Lord your God has apportioned to all the nations under heaven'. However, this is not astrology it is astronomy that we are looking at here. The Magi, who were mathematicians, astrologers and astronomers, knew what this star meant and like Daniel who was the Chief Magi before them, they were focussed on the Messiah and were interested in the prophecy concerning his birth as the King of Kings.

I see a link here between Daniel, the Magi and the Essenes, they were all interested in astronomy, were vegetarian and opposed to animal sacrifices, what some may call today New Age. They are all peoples who were seeking God, interested in prophecy, experienced dreams, signs and wonders. The Christian mystics emerging in this day and age are similar in aspirations, they are seeking wisdom and truth, to experience the presence of God, seeking to engage with God, and to know heaven on earth. They are breaking out of the matrix of religious lies. I believe that the New Age were certainly on to something, and the mystics of today are no longer fearful of some of the practices that developed starting in the 1970s in Western nations in this movement, in fact they are beginning to use some of the healing and holistic forms of medicine practised by them.

I have always preferred natural alternative remedies, but have had disapproval from Christian friends, and so kept quiet about using such things as aromatherapy pure essential oils, herbal remedies and so on. I threw books away which I had read, by authors like Louise Hay who wrote The Power is Within You, and Everyday Positive Thinking. I think I read all the positive thinking books on the market, and spent years turning myself into a positive thinker. What is wrong with that? Nothing! The work I did then has helped me enormously in my spiritual development in recent years, and actually much of it is founded on Biblical truths, such as the renewal of the mind, as in Romans 12:2, where Paul urges his brothers to, 'be transformed by the renewing of your mind'. Another well-known book was called The Power of Now by Eckhart Tolle, actually a very useful and helpful book, about living in the present, again the principles are good. I read a lot of self-help books, another famous one is Feel the Fear and Do it Anyway, I learnt a lot from these so called 'New Age' books. I also did a course at Cardiff University on Mindfulness and Meditation, considered 'New Age' at the time, but now Christians are beginning to see the value in these techniques and are no longer fearful of them.

God has good things in store for humanity and I believe that is what we are stepping into now. For me, one of the signs of this is the movement towards a more sustainable lifestyle nationally, globally and individually. The aspect that I am optimistic and excited about is the huge move towards veganism and vegetarianism, especially amongst young people. More and more people are switching to a plant-based diet, not just individuals, but cafes and restaurants: the vegetarian section in supermarkets has grown, even farmers are turning to crop farming. It was reported in the Daily Mail on 2 January 2020 that, 'The soaring popularity of vegan and vegetarian diets saw meat sales drop by almost £185 million last year. Celebrities from Bill Clinton to Benedict Cumberbatch have been at the forefront of the switch away from meat, which is having a dramatic impact on people's shopping choices'. It also said that, 'Most people cite a healthier lifestyle as the main driver of their decision to turn vegan, although animal welfare and protecting the environment are also influential'. These changes are happening rapidly, and it is not a mere temporary fad, it is the way forward, it is unstoppable, what was a fringe movement is becoming mainstream. I believe it is just one aspect of the restoration of all things that God promises in Acts 3:21. Christians, however, are lagging behind in this, though I am finding that more and more Christian Mystics are embracing a plant-based lifestyle, asking questions and seeking Biblical grounds for doing so.

The Lord says, in Isaiah 43, "See, I am doing a new thing! Now it springs up; do you not perceive it? I am making a way in the desert and streams in the wasteland". In Ezekiel 36, 34-35, the Lord promises, 'The desolate land will be cultivated instead of lying desolate in the sight of all who pass through it. They will say, "This land that has laid waste has become like the garden of Eden; the cities that were lying in ruins, desolate and destroyed are now fortified and inhabited".'

God has promised to bless His people, Israel, He will bless Jerusalem. Israel is already being blessed. It is one of the most resilient and technologically advanced market economies in the world. The country leads in innovative industries such as high-tech and cleantech, and is a world leader in advanced agricultural methods. They are the world leaders in wastewater to agriculture reuse with ninety percent of all domestic water being used for agriculture. They have developed the most sophisticated way of growing leaf crops using hydroponic and aquaponic greenhouses that work by pumping just the right amount of nutrients and water directly to the plants' roots. They also invented drip irrigation, which is now used all round the world.

There is an abundance of high-quality fresh fruit and vegetables growing in the land, much of it grown organically, which is reflected in the brightness of colour and flavour. In 2018 it was reported in the Independent that Tel Aviv is the vegan capital of the world, with 400 vegan and vegan-friendly kitchens catering to most of Israel's 200,000 vegans.

In Zechariah 8: 12-13, the Lord Almighty declares, "The seed will grow well, the vine will yield its fruit, the ground will produce its crops, and the heavens will drop their dew. I will give all these things as an inheritance to the remnant of this people. As you have been an object of cursing among the nations, O Judah and Israel, so will I save you, and you will be a blessing". Israel is a hugely innovative and advanced nation way ahead of the rest of the world, and so is being blessed by God in these times, as the prophets declared it would happen. Amos 9: 13-15 also talks about this restoration of all things,

"New wine will drip from the mountains
And flow from all the hills.
I will bring back my exiled people Israel;
They will rebuild the ruined cities and live in them.
They will plant vineyards and drink their wine;
They will make gardens and eat their fruit.
I will plant Israel in their own land,
Never again to be uprooted
From the land I have given them," says the Lord your God.

All of these things are happening now. The promised restoration of all things, I believe, includes many aspects of our lives, it is also a spiritual restoration for us as individuals. For example, Joel tells us that the years the locusts have eaten will be repaid. Any category of loss that has occurred in our lives, God will restore, years lost perhaps because of a bad relationship, bad parents, bad decisions, lack of faith, lack of knowledge, and so on. He restores my soul (Psalm 23), I am being renewed and healed daily. God has promised the renewal of all things to us, Eden restored. In Romans 8 Paul tells us creation groans for its redemption, and this of course, includes the earth and all of His amazing creatures.

Part of the Lord's prayer says, '… thy kingdom come, thy will be done, on earth as it is in Heaven'. I do not believe there is death or killing going on in Heaven. God's kingdom is being established and all of creation is groaning waiting eagerly for the sons of God to be revealed. (Romans 8:19)

The beautiful verses in Isaiah 11:6-9 depict a future Peaceable Kingdom:

The wolf will live with the lamb, the leopard will lie down with the goat, the calf and the lion and the yearling together; and a little child will lead them.

The cow will feed with the bear, their young will lie down together, and the lion will eat straw like the ox.

The infant will play near the hole of the cobra, and the young child put his hand into the viper's nest,

They will neither harm nor destroy on all my holy mountain, for the earth will be full of the knowledge of the Lord as the waters cover the sea.

I think the Peaceable Kingdom is beginning to happen now. In fact, I believe future generations, perhaps in the next ten to twenty years, will see rapid changes in people's diet. There is an openness and a rising awareness among the population and nations worldwide that we need to eat less meat, I would even go so far as to say that we will see an end to eating animals for food in the very near future. The vegan musician Bryan Adams has recently said that he believes killing animals for food is destroying the planet, and it will be a thing of the past. The younger generation are currently taking the lead. As a child I would not eat meat, from a very early age I remember refusing to eat turkey at Christmas, instinctively knowing that the nicely carved white meat on the plate was, in reality, a dead bird. Somewhere within my consciousness and conscience was a deep repulsion at the very thought of eating this dead flesh.

I believe the gift of love and compassion towards animals was given to me by God. He has put this passion in my heart. My God-given sensibilities and sensitivities towards animals, which constitute my very being as a person, prevent me from tolerating suffering in both animals and humans and I believe that God's creation has a meaning and worth beyond mere human use, abuse and utility.

We see the young sixteen-year-old Greta Thunberg of Sweden leading the way in the environmental campaign which has swept the world and caught the attention of the media and her contemporaries. Her passion is to be admired as a next generation leader and role model.

I believe the same instinct I had at a young age against eating dead flesh is in many young people, and is buried deep inside us all, just as imagination is an innate gift which we bring into the world with us, but the systems of the world soon repress these instincts as we succumb and conform to society and the status quo. But that is thankfully changing. God's kingdom will be established on earth as it is in heaven.

As Christians, I believe we have a responsibility to partner with God in bringing heaven to earth. Clearly, we are in a new season, a new age spiritually, where our faith is all about intimacy with God, about encountering, drawing on and releasing the power and love of God. The love of God transforms, heals and saves the world. We are moving from passivity and compromise in the church and it is a radical shift.

I believe a love for all of God's creation needs to be part of this shake up within and outside the church. We need an understanding of God that includes animals. In Psalm 148 we see all of creation including sea creatures, beasts and all cattle, creeping things and flying fowl, praising the Lord. 'Let them praise the Lord, for He commanded and they were created'. The abundance of beauty and variety in God's creation constantly blows my mind. It displays His majestic glory and amazing creativity. I believe that animal life and animal suffering does matter to God.

It is a mass consciousness and conventional thinking, and a tendency to lull our conscience by a series or shuffling excuses that has duped us into thinking it's okay to participate in death and eat dead flesh. There is much debate about the environment and climate change and there are reams of articles on the subject written by academics. But humans are in a dilemma, deep down they know that one of the answers lies in cutting down or even eliminating the consumption of livestock. The first item on the BBC news on 8 August 2019 declared that United Nations scientists were calling for a switch to plant-based food. They had concluded in a climate change report prepared for the UN's Intergovernmental Panel on Climate Change, that a plant-based diet can fight climate change and that the West's high consumption of meat and dairy produce is fuelling global warming. They said that more people could be fed using less land if individuals cut down on eating meat, but they stopped short of calling on everyone to become vegetarian or vegan.

We need to open our eyes, trust our heart and review our eating habits. The massacre of animals to appease our greed and gluttony cannot go on. The act of slaughtering an innocent animal is a violent, horrific and primitive act which brutalises the worker who carries out the execution and is corrupting society.

I am not a conservationist and I acknowledge that we need to change our lifestyles for the sake of our environment and the planet. But my own personal and primary concern has been for the welfare of animals who share our world. It is God's right that the creatures He created and values are cared for with love and compassion by us. We need to listen to the voice in our own heart.

APPENDIX

Some Biblical Verses concerning Animal Sacrifice

Jeremiah 6:20 Your burnt offerings are not acceptable, nor your sacrifices sweet to me.

Jeremiah 7:21-26 Add your burnt offerings to your sacrifices and eat meat. For I did not speak to your fathers, or command them in the day that I bought them out of the land of Egypt, concerning burnt offerings or sacrifices. But this is what I commanded them, saying, 'Obey my voice, and I will be your God.'

Isaiah 1:11 To what purpose is the multitude of your sacrifices to me? Says the Lord. I have had enough of burnt offerings of rams. And the fat of fed cattle. I do not delight in the blood of bulls, or of lambs or goats.

Isaiah 1:13 Bring me more futile sacrifices; incense is an abomination to me.

Isaiah 66:3 He who kills a bull is as if he slays a man; he who sacrifices a lamb, as if he breaks a dog's neck; he who offers a grain offering, as if he offers swine's blood; he who burns incense, as I he blesses an idol.

Hosea 6:6 For I desire mercy and not sacrifice, and the knowledge of God more than burnt offerings.

Hosea 8:13 For the sacrifices of My offerings they sacrifice flesh and eat it, but the Lord does not accept them.

Micah 6:6 Shall I come before Him with burnt offerings, with calves a year old? Will the Lord be pleased with thousands of rams, ten thousand rivers of oil? Shall I give my firstborn for my transgressions. The fruit of my body for the sin of my soul. He has shown you O man, what is good; and what does the Lord require of you but to do justly, to love mercy, and to walk humbly with your God?

Psalm 40:6 Sacrifice and offering You did not desire; my ears you have opened. Burnt offerings and sin offering You did not require. Then I said, "Behold I come; in the scroll of the book it is written of me. I delight to do Your will, O my God, and Your law is within my heart."

Psalm 51: 16-17 For You do not desire sacrifice, or else I would give it; You do not delight in burnt offering. The sacrifices of God are a broken spirit, a broken and contrite heart. These, O God, You will not despise.

Amos 21 I hate, I despise your feast days, And I do not savour your sacred assemblies.

Amos 22 Though you offer me burnt offerings and your grain offerings, I will not accept them, nor will I regard your fattened peace offerings.

Hebrews 10: 1-10 (read all of it) v3 In those sacrifices there is a reminder of sin every year. For it is not possible that the blood of bulls and goats could take away sins.
V5 Therefore, when He came into the world, He said: "Sacrifice and offering You did not desire, but a body you have prepared for me. In burnt offerings and sacrifices for sin You had no pleasure.

References and Recommended Reading

Linzey, Andrew, Reverend Professor, *Animal Theology* (SCM Press Ltd, London, 1994)

------ *Why Animal Suffering Matters, Philosophy, Theology, and Practical Ethics* (Oxford University Press, 2009)

Singer, Peter, *Practical Ethics* (Cambridge University Press, 1994)

------- *Animal Liberation* (Jonathan Cape, London, 1990)

Salt, Henry, *Animals' Rights, Considered in Relation to Social Progress* (Centaur Press Ltd, London, 1980)

Regan, Tom and Linzey, Andrew, *Animals and Christianity, A Book of Readings* (SPCK, London, 1988)

Scully, Matthew, *Dominion, The Power of Man, the Suffering of Animals, and the Call to Mercy* (St Martin's Griffin, New York, 2002)

Masson, Jeffrey Moussaieff, *The Face on your Plate, The Truth about Food* (W. W. Norton & Company, New York and London, 2009)

Webb, Stephen H., *On God and Dogs, A Christian Theology of Compassion for Animals* (Oxford University Press, 1998)

Turner, E. S., *All Heaven in a Rage* (Centaur Press, Fontwell, Sussex, 1992)

Boone, J. Allen, *Kinship with all Life* (Harper Collins, 1954)

Linzey, Andrew Ed., *The Link Between Animal Abuse and Human Violence* (Sussex Academic Press, 2009)

Carter, Christopher Paul, *Cosmic Shift, A New Season of Faith*, (Fig and Vine Publishing, 2015)

Printed in Great Britain
by Amazon

64706413R00061